Samuel French Acting Edition

Everything is Wonderful

by Chelsea Marcantel

SAMUELFRENCH.COM   SAMUELFRENCH.CO.UK

FOR PRODUCTION ENQUIRIES

UNITED STATES AND CANADA
Info@SamuelFrench.com
1-866-598-8449

UNITED KINGDOM AND EUROPE
Plays@SamuelFrench.co.uk
020-7255-4302

Each title is subject to availability from Samuel French, depending upon country of performance. Please be aware that *EVERYTHING IS WONDERFUL* may not be licensed by Samuel French in your territory. Professional and amateur producers should contact the nearest Samuel French office or licensing partner to verify availability.

MUSIC USE NOTE

Licensees are solely responsible for obtaining formal written permission from copyright owners to use copyrighted music in the performance of this play and are strongly cautioned to do so. If no such permission is obtained by the licensee, then the licensee must use only original music that the licensee owns and controls. Licensees are solely responsible and liable for all music clearances and shall indemnify the copyright owners of the play(s) and their licensing agent, Samuel French, against any costs, expenses, losses and liabilities arising from the use of music by licensees. Please contact the appropriate music licensing authority in your territory for the rights to any incidental music.

IMPORTANT BILLING AND CREDIT REQUIREMENTS

If you have obtained performance rights to this title, please refer to your licensing agreement for important billing and credit requirements.

EVERYTHING IS WONDERFUL received developmental support from the Juilliard School, The New Colony, Montana Repertory Theatre, and Atlantic Theater Company.

EVERYTHING IS WONDERFUL premiered at the Contemporary American Theater Festival in Shepherdstown, West Virginia (Ed Herendeen, Artistic Director) on July 7, 2017. The production was directed by Ed Herendeen, with set design by David M. Barber, lighting design by D.M. Wood, costume design by Therese Bruck, and sound design and original music by Miles Polaski. The production stage manager was Debra A. Acquavella and the stage manager was Tina Shackleford. The cast was as follows:

MIRI . . . . Jessica Savage
ERIC . . . . Jason Babinsky
ABRAM . . . . Lucky Gretzinger
RUTH . . . . Lexi Lapp
ESTHER . . . . Hollis McCarthy
JACOB . . . . Paul DeBoy

CHARACTERS

MIRI – Twenty-five years old in the present. Smart, plain-spoken, independent. Left the Amish at the age of twenty and coped by building a hard shell around her heart. More like her mother than her father.

ERIC – Late thirties/early forties. Unemployed, confused, and adrift in the world. He is an addict, and there is a dark core at the center of him that he's fighting very hard to keep buried. Deeply self-centered and self-loathing. Has a hard time finishing a sentence; when he changes directions mid-thought, that moment is indicated by *(No...)* in the script.

ABRAM – Twenty-five years old in the present. Strapping, polite, charming, and entitled. Clean-shaven to indicate he is an unmarried Amish man. Miri's childhood sweetheart and also the reason she left the Amish. He is a very charming brute; the audience should like him.

RUTH – Eighteen years old in the present. Miri's youngest sibling and a version of Miri as she might have been as a "good Amish girl." Ruth is sweet and good, but not simple. Unintentionally funny in spite of herself. More like her father than her mother.

ESTHER – Late forties/early fifties in the present. Miri's mother. A hard worker who suffers no fools and speaks her mind, and lives with a hereditary current of anger just below the surface. On the outside she seems simple and perhaps submissive, but she has a core of steel.

JACOB – *(Pronounced: YAK-ob)* Late forties/early fifties in the present. Miri's father, an open and earnest man. Wears the distinctive short beard sans mustache that indicates a married Amish man. Believes the best way to make peace with the deaths of his children is to actively work on forgiveness. The tragedy has made him desperate to reconcile with his oldest daughter.

SETTING

The play takes place in both the present and the past, in a series of suggested locations in and around an Amish community. If possible, a clothesline hung with dark, traditional plainclothes can be strung across the space to give a sense of place. Some of these locations appear onstage simultaneously; locations do not always appear in the same spot onstage. The action should flow fluidly from one space to the next without stopping. Light and sound should be used to suggest these locations, as well as minimal, consistent props and set pieces. No blackouts, please, except at the end of Act One.

List of Locations

The living room

The front porch

In front of a convenience store on the edge of town

The field behind the house

The kitchen

A barn

The woods

AUTHOR'S NOTES

Transitions

Within the six larger movements, scenes overlap and move in and out of each other without a pause. Between each of the six larger movements there should be a moment of emotional reset – a bare stage, a deep breath, a few seconds of reset.

Accents

At home, most of the characters in this play speak Pennsylvania Dutch, a dialect of German. When speaking English, these characters have a specific Germanic accent – Esther and Jacob's accents are strongest, Ruth and Abram's accents are less pronounced, Miri's accent is almost gone, and Eric has no accent at all. Actors are encouraged to use a light but specific hand with the accents.

Physicality

As a general rule, the characters should not touch each other. When it is indicated by the script that they do, the touch should be *a big moment.* Also, the physicality of the Amish characters, who have spent their lives working in their bodies, should be markedly different from the physicality of Eric, who has spent his life working in his head.

Words

The phonetic word **te** is sometimes used in place of "the." It is pronounced "tuh."

The phonetic word **tat** is sometimes used in place of "that." It is pronounced "taht."

The word **Dat** is the Amish equivalent of "Daddy" and rhymes with "bat."

The word **English** is used by the Amish as a noun and an adjective, to describe non-Amish Americans (because we speak English).

Dialogue between Amish characters should be even and steady, but not overly slow. Dialogue between Miri and Eric should be noticeably faster, and Miri should speak more quickly in the present than she does in the past.

ACT ONE

Scene One: Sweet Tooth

(Present day. The play opens in the living room of a spare but large Amish home. It is the end of a long day of work, and ESTHER *and* JACOB *sit together in silence, taking care of little chores. It is one week since the accident; this is the first time they've been alone together since their sons died.* ESTHER *is mending one of her husband's shirts.* JACOB *is oiling a leather bridle.)*

JACOB. Benny was a sweet name, but tat was an argumentative horse. New horse is gentle. Has an amenable demeanor. *(Pause.)* Think I'm goin' to name te new horse Honey.

ESTHER. *(Without looking up.)* Ruth will want to name te new horse.

JACOB. Ruth will like te name "Honey."

(They sit in silence together for a moment.)

I've spoken to Abram. He's arranged for John and Samuel to help us in te field for te rest of te month.

ESTHER. Tat will make things easier.

JACOB. I have been concerned, Esther. I feel so tired.

ESTHER. *(Softly.)* I feel tired, too.

JACOB. Abram told me tat Rebekah and Elizabeth have offered to help with your work, and Ruth's.

ESTHER. They have. But we're managin' just fine.

JACOB. I don't want to manage. Don't want to feel like we're just gettin' by. Want things to get better.

ESTHER. *(Finally looking up at him.)* Things are gettin' better. Abram will send his brothers to help in te field for te rest of te month, and you'll catch up with te work.

JACOB. What about next month?

ESTHER. "Sufficient unto te day is te trouble thereof."

JACOB. *(Sharply.)* I'd say our day's trouble is sufficient. Yes, I would say tat.

ESTHER. Don't be angry, Jacob.

JACOB. Not angry. I'm tired.

ESTHER. And everythin' I'm sayin' is makin' you more tired. I can see tat.

JACOB. Apologize for raisin' my voice.

ESTHER. *(Putting her hand on his, gently.)* Everythin' is hard right now, I know. But He will see us through.

JACOB. Tell myself tat some days, and it helps. Today it did not.

> *(Beat.)*
>
> **(ESTHER** *looks at him in silence.)*

(Backing off.) Everythin' is wonderful.

> *(There is a moment of silence, then a knock at the door.* **JACOB** *looks at* **ESTHER** *in mild surprise, then rises to answer the knock. He opens the door to the small room, and* **ERIC** *enters, pale as a ghost and instantly, egregiously out of place. No one says anything. It feels – now, and for the rest of the scene – like* **JACOB** *might strike* **ERIC** *at any moment. There is a long silence.)*

(With enormous control.) Good evenin', young man.

> **(ERIC** *cannot say anything. He just nods.)*

Would you like to come in?

> **(ERIC** *nods again.)*

This is my wife. Esther.

(**ERIC** *nods at her, then hangs his head.*)

Won't you sit down?

ERIC. *(Cracking.)* I'm sorry.

JACOB. *(Betraying nothing.)* Would you like some lemonade? Our Ruth made it this afternoon.

ERIC. I'm sorry! *(It's all he can say.)*

JACOB. I made tat chair. It's a good chair. Sit down.

ERIC. I'm sorry.

JACOB. Me too. Sit down.

ERIC. I'm sorry.

JACOB. Please. Sit.

ERIC. I can't.

JACOB. We forgave you. In te hospital.

ERIC. Don't.

JACOB. I met your father. At te hospital. Don't know if he mentioned tat?

> (**ERIC** *sits.*)

> (*Lights up on a different portion of the stage – the front of an English convenience store not far away, the same evening.* **ABRAM** *is there with two candy bars in one hand, opening them.* **RUTH** *enters and sees him. He freezes. She stares.*)

Please say whatever you need to say.

ERIC. *(Struggling.)* I didn't see it. *(No...)* I wasn't looking. *(No...)* I was looking at the sun. *(No...)* I couldn't see it. Which is ridiculous, because it was so big. And right in front of me.

ESTHER. What is it we can do for you?

ERIC. Press charges.

> (*There is a short silence.*)

ABRAM. Good evenin', Ruth.

RUTH. Good evenin', Abram.

ABRAM. You're lookin' well.

ERIC. I was falling asleep and the sun was in my eyes and I was feeling okay, or nothing, for once. And I wasn't drunk, not really, not legally, and so the state's not... But I *should* go to jail. I should, for this. Something should happen to me!

JACOB. *(Pause.)* Maybe something will.

> *(Lights dim on the living room.* **JACOB**, **ERIC**, *and* **ESTHER** *exit.)*

RUTH. Are you –

ABRAM. *(Interrupting.)* What brings you to town?

RUTH. Oh! A letter. I have a letter to mail.

ABRAM. Oh? To whom?

RUTH. Whom...?

ABRAM. To whom are you writin', Ruth?

RUTH. *(Cagey.)* Ah. *(Motioning to his hand.)* You have a sweet tooth?

ABRAM. *(Slightly embarrassed.)* Yes. It's... It's nice to see you. How is your mother?

RUTH. She's...she is...as you might expect.

ABRAM. I've arranged for John and Samuel to work with your dat this month. I'll be able to help out more myself, soon as the Yoders' barn is finished.

RUTH. Very kind of you.

ABRAM. Levi and Joshua were... They were almost brothers to me.

RUTH. Yes. Suppose so.

> *(A short pause.)*

ABRAM. I'll be seein' you then, soon. At your farm.

RUTH. Uh-huh. *(She turns to leave, but turns back.)* Your secret is safe with me.

ABRAM. My secret?

RUTH. The sweets. I won't tell anyone.

ABRAM. I appreciate that. I won't tell anyone I saw you mailin' that letter.

RUTH. *(Smiling.)* Nice runnin' into you, Abram.

> *(Something has been set in motion.)*
>
> *(**RUTH** exits. **MIRI** enters.)*
>
> *(Shift –> The Past.)*
>
> *(We've gone back in time ten years, as indicated by a sound and light cue. **MIRI** rides in [shakily] on a simple, old bicycle. She is dressed in Amish plainclothes. We are still in front of the convenience store.)*

MIRI. *(Seeing the candy bars.)* Aha! Caught you! What's that in your hand?

ABRAM. In my hand? Who cares what's in my hand? What's *this*?

MIRI. *(Slowly, patronizingly.)* This is called a bicycle, Abram.

ABRAM. I know *what* it is. Is it yours?

MIRI. *(Proudly.)* All mine!

ABRAM. Where'd you get it?

MIRI. The English family up the road, they're havin' a rummage sale. I bargained for it.

ABRAM. How much?

MIRI. Clean their house three times this month.

ABRAM. That's practically for free!

MIRI. I know!

ABRAM. Where'd you plan to hide it?

MIRI. Hide it? I plan to ride it!

ABRAM. The bishop's wife don't like bicycles.

MIRI. Bishop's wife ain't the bishop, and the bishop hasn't forbidden bicycles.

ABRAM. Your mama will be madder than a wet hen.

MIRI. Dat will let me keep it. I'm nearly fifteen. Mama won't be able to say nothin'.

(A short pause. They stare at each other, both extremely excited.)

ABRAM. Let me ride it.

MIRI. Maybe one day.

ABRAM. Today!

MIRI. I just got it!

ABRAM. You have to give it to me. You're my –

MIRI. *(Interrupting.)* Nothin'! I'm your nothin'.

ABRAM. Well, you will be one day.

MIRI. *(With mock haughtiness.)* I barely know you.

ABRAM. You will be one day and everyone says it.

MIRI. Well I'm not your nothin' yet.

ABRAM. You should submit the bicycle to me for practice. For one day.

MIRI. *(Flattered, but embarrassed.)* Whatever you're talkin' about is a long way off.

> *(Lights up on **RUTH** as she enters the kitchen with a stack of plates. She begins to set the table. She has five plates, but she sets four places.)*

ABRAM. *(Getting closer to **MIRI**.)* Not that far off. I bet you'll be married by the time you're eighteen.

MIRI. You'll have to catch me first. I'm faster than you, with this.

ABRAM. You'll go cruisin' down the road and your cap strings will come untied, and you'll forget to tie them back, and someone will see you. You'll be in trouble with the bishop in the hour.

MIRI. I'm always in trouble with the bishop anyways.

(Climbing off the bike, teasing him.) Where'd you get the candies, Abram? Been to town today? Maybe to the English movies again?

> *(**ABRAM** jumps on the bike and rides off, badly.)*

ABRAM. You can't prove it!

MIRI. *(Screaming.)* Come back! Hey, come back here!

RUTH. *(Looking at* **MIRI.***)* Hey, come back here.

MIRI. *(Startled, she looks across to* **RUTH.***)* Ruth?

RUTH. *(To* **MIRI.***)* Hey, come back here.

> (**MIRI** *stares at* **RUTH.** **RUTH** *stares back.* **ERIC** *enters the kitchen.*)
>
> *(Shift –> The Present.)*
>
> *(As indicated by a sound and light cue.)*
>
> (**ESTHER** *and* **JACOB** *enter the kitchen.*)

ESTHER. Ruth?

> *(The spell is broken.* **MIRI** *exits.)*

JACOB. Eric will be joinin' us for supper. *(Pause.)* Set a place for Eric.

ERIC. *(Sheepishly.)* I don't... I don't eat meat, if...

> *(A short beat. They stare at him.)*

JACOB. There are plenty of biscuits and vegetables. You won't go hungry.

ERIC. Okay.

> *(There is a short silence.* **ESTHER** *and* **RUTH** *sit.)*

Is there another guest?

ESTHER. No. *(Coolly.)* Te Lord only blessed us with four children.

> (**JACOB** *sits.*)

JACOB. Levi and Joshua have gone on to their reward. They were good boys.

ESTHER. Miriam has just gone on.

RUTH. But we always set her place.

JACOB. And we always have room for a guest. *(Pointedly.)* More room than ever.

> (**ERIC** *sits.*)
>
> (**JACOB** *reaches out his hand to take* **ERIC**'s *for the dinner blessing.*)

(**ERIC** *hesitates, then accepts.*)

(*Shift –> The Past.*)

(*As indicated by a sound and light cue.*)

(*We are in the living room, five years before.*)

JACOB. Do you confess to actin' worldly?

MIRI. Yes.

JACOB. Do you confess to puttin' yourself before your community, and testin' the ways of te *Ordnung*?

MIRI. Yes.

JACOB. Do you confess to te sins of pride and disobedience, tat sunder us all from God?

MIRI. Yes. I confess these things. And I repent them.

JACOB. Do you repent tat you have held on to anger, tat you have allowed this anger to turn to vanity?

MIRI. Vanity? No.

JACOB. Confess it.

MIRI. I will not.

JACOB. Forgiveness is te spine of life. If you cannot practice reconciliation, you put us all at risk.

MIRI. Am I not at risk, Dat?

(*A beat.*)

JACOB. In Germany, and in Switzerland, they persecuted us and martyred us. And now, here, they mock us, close our schools, try to draft us for their wars, (*Pause.*) kill and kidnap our children. And we forgive. Always, we forgive.

MIRI. How?

JACOB. We do this te same way we do everything. *Gelassenheit.*

MIRI. "Submission."

JACOB. Submission is a bad word to the English. Their lives are built around grabbin' and holdin' on. Our lives are not our own.

(A silence between them. **JACOB** *looks at his daughter, sees how broken she is.)*

(Fervently.) I suffered what you suffered, just not in te same way. But I must surrender my right to revenge. I must surrender my right to anger and resentment and self-pity.

MIRI. And rage.

JACOB. Bad things happen. They happen quite a lot. And surrender is not te only way to move on. But it is te way we know best. I wish I could show you an easier path, but I have not found one. You must, you MUST let go of te thing inside you tat makes you want to crush him. It's a curse. I am tryin' to take this hardness off your heart, girl. Speak, forgive, forget.

MIRI. How can I forgive him? Just like that? It won't fix the way I feel. It won't make anything right.

JACOB. Forgiveness and reconciliation are two different things, Miri. Forgiveness is a choice. It happens in an instant. Reconciliation is a journey. It may take you the rest of your life. But forgiveness must come first.

(Shift -> The Present.)

(The scene shifts to the front porch. **JACOB** *and* **ERIC** *stand outside the front door.)*

(They are both very still, and very unsure.)

ERIC. Thanks again, for dinner. It was really good. I'm sorry about that whole...meat...thing... *(No...)* I don't know why I –

JACOB. *(Interrupting.)* You came on a bus?

ERIC. Yes, sir.

(Silence.)

JACOB. It's late.

ERIC. Yes, sir.

(Silence.)

JACOB. Don't want to put you on the road at this hour. *(Short pause.)* But I can't have you sleepin' in our home. Ruth's unmarried. Wouldn't be right.

ERIC. No, of course.

JACOB. Te barn will be plenty warm tonight. There are a few quilts in te hayloft you can sleep on. Very pleasant. Spent a few nights out there myself over te years.

ERIC. Oh. Okay, yeah. Great.

JACOB. In te mornin', we'll see what we can do for you.

> *(JACOB turns to exit.)*

ERIC. I can't... *(No...)* What will...

JACOB. *(Interrupting, convincing himself.)* It's no mistake, you comin' to us this evenin'. Everythin' happens by God's providence.

> *(ERIC and JACOB exit to the barn.)*
>
> *(Shift -> The Past.)*
>
> *(ESTHER and MIRI enter. They are in the living room, five years ago.)*

ESTHER. We don't think you're wrong. To feel this way. We all understand, we just wish you'd change your mind.

MIRI. Change my mind?

ESTHER. Give it time.

MIRI. I have given it time!

ESTHER. Only a few months! You're so young. Time heals all wounds.

MIRI. I should wait until I want to kill myself?

ESTHER. Never say such a thing!

MIRI. Just pretend to forget, like everyone else?

ESTHER. Don't pretend. Do forget. God will heal you, if you give Him time. Impatience is disrespectful. You always had a disrespectful leanin'.

MIRI. Disrespectful? What happened can stop happenin' to him. It can't stop happenin' to me.

ESTHER. We shouldn't even be talkin' about this.

MIRI. Everyone smiles at him, they shake his hand. They say it's my fault, behind my back.

ESTHER. Abram has been forgiven.

MIRI. *I* can't forgive him. And that doesn't even matter!

ESTHER. Have you thought about your soul, Miriam? Have you thought about eternity in hell?

MIRI. Believe me, Mama. I have thought a long time about hell.

ESTHER. I'm offerin' you comfort, and you're offerin' me petulance and disrespect. *(Pause.)* Look at me and tell me. Tell me you never want to see me again.

*(A short pause. **RUTH** joins them in the past.)*

RUTH. What's goin' on?

ESTHER. Your sister is leavin' us. She never wants to see you again.

RUTH. Miri?

MIRI. *(To **RUTH**.)* You're so good at it. I'm not.

RUTH. Don't leave! You're baptized –

MIRI. *(Interrupting.)* Please, Ruth. You'll make this so awful if you keep talkin'.

RUTH. I'm angry right now. With you. I'm really angry.

*(**MIRI** crosses to **RUTH** and puts her hand on **RUTH**'s shoulder.)*

MIRI. I'm leavin' in the mornin'. I have to, Ruth.

*(**RUTH** begins to cry, silently. A moment passes.)*

ESTHER. *(At great cost to herself.)* Why don't you leave now?

*(**MIRI** stares at her mother for a moment, then exits.)*

*(To **RUTH**.)* Don't cry.

*(**ESTHER** does not move to comfort **RUTH**. Lights dim on the living room.)*

(There is a sound and light cue to indicate transition into the next movement.)

Scene Two: Toil

(The Past and Present.)

(The following is stylized movement, not a naturalistic enactment. Over the course of the song, a week passes.)

(Lights up on **JACOB** *working in the field with a shovel. After a moment,* **ERIC** *enters, sees what* **JACOB** *is doing, and watches him.* **JACOB** *looks over at* **ERIC**, *exits, and returns with a second shovel, which he hands to* **ERIC**. *Nothing is said.* **JACOB** *goes back to work.* **ERIC** *begins to imitate the work, poorly.)*

(They work for a few moments and then lights come up on **ESTHER** *cooking in the kitchen on another part of the stage. She does this alone for a few moments; the noises of her work with pots and pans mingle with the noises of the shovels almost musically.)*

(They go on working like this for a few moments, and then lights come up on **RUTH** *and* **MIRI** *[in her Amish plainclothes] scrubbing the porch. They are ten years in the past. The noises of their brushes at work mingle with their mother's and the men's almost musically.)*

(Lights indicate that the girls are in the past.)

(After a moment, the work inspires **RUTH** *to begin singing a hymn.*)*

RUTH.

EACH DAY I'LL DO / A GOLDEN DEED
BY HELPIN' THOSE / WHO ARE IN NEED.
MY LIFE ON EARTH / IS BUT A SPAN
AND SO I'LL DO / THE BEST I CAN.

---

*Licensees should use the melody from the 1918 William M. Golden hymn "A Beautiful Life."

(JACOB joins in the singing. It becomes a call-and-response, with JACOB leading.)

JACOB & RUTH.

LIFE'S EVENIN' SUN
    LIFE'S EVENIN' SUN
IS SINKIN' LOW
    IS SINKIN' LOW
A FEW MORE DAYS
    A FEW MORE DAYS
AND I MUST GO.
    AND I MUST GO.

(ESTHER joins in the singing. She joins RUTH's part.)

JACOB, RUTH & ESTHER.

TO MEET THE DEEDS
    TO MEET THE DEEDS
THAT I HAVE DONE
    THAT I HAVE DONE
WHERE THERE WILL BE
    WHERE THERE WILL BE
NO SETTIN' SUN.
    NO SETTIN' SUN.

(MIRI joins in the singing. She joins the response with RUTH and ESTHER. They go on working and singing until the song is nearly done, but they are interrupted by the entrance of ABRAM.)

JACOB, RUTH, ESTHER & MIRI.

I'LL HELP SOMEONE
    I'LL HELP SOMEONE
IN TIME OF NEED
    IN TIME OF NEED
AND JOURNEY ON
    AND JOURNEY ON
WITH RAPID SPEED.
    WITH RAPID SPEED.
I'LL HELP THE SICK

I'LL HELP THE SICK
AND POOR AND WEAK
       AND POOR AND WEAK
AND WORDS OF KIND–
       AND WORDS OF KIND–
–NESS TO THEM SPEAK.
       –NESS TO THEM SPEAK.
LIFE'S EVENIN' SUN
       LIFE'S EVENIN' SUN
IS SINKIN' LOW
       IS SINKIN' LOW
A FEW MORE DAYS
       A FEW MORE DAYS
AND I MUST GO
       AND I MUST GO

    (In unison.)

TO MEET THE DEEDS
THAT I HAVE DONE
WHERE THERE WILL BE / NO SET–

> (**ABRAM** *enters at the same part of the stage where* **JACOB** *and* **ERIC** *are working. As soon as he enters, all singing and noise-making stops abruptly.*)

JACOB. Hello, Abram.

ABRAM. Good afternoon, Jacob. It's good to see you.

> (**JACOB** *subtly motions with his head for* **ERIC** *to leave.* **ERIC** *gets the hint.*)

ERIC. *(Nodding to the men.)* Um, excuse me.

> (**ERIC** *exits.*)

JACOB. Somethin' I can do for you today, Abram?

ABRAM. Came by to see if I could be of any help to *you*, Jacob.

JACOB. We're managin'. Your brothers have been helpin' out. And Eric, for te last few days.

ABRAM. Eric. The English one that just left?

JACOB. Yes. Te English.

ABRAM. Doesn't look like much help. Doesn't know how to hold a shovel.

JACOB. He's learnin'.

ABRAM. How did he come to be sleepin' in your barn, Jacob?

JACOB. *(Pause.)* Do you want to know, or does te bishop?

ABRAM. *(Carefully.)* We all want to know how you're doin'. You, and Esther, and Ruth.

JACOB. Eric is...te English. Te driver.

ABRAM. The driver? Of the car?

JACOB. Yes. He came to us.

ABRAM. And you took him in? To work?

JACOB. Both of my sons have died. My *sons*. And here is a young man who wants to do their work. He's not my son, but he does te work.

ABRAM. You really think that what you're doin' is God's will?

JACOB. It's not mine to say what's God's will. It's only mine to say what's in front of me.

ABRAM. What's in front of you is the man who hit your sons with his car. And killed them.

> *(A beat between them.)*

JACOB. Te day after te accident, as soon as Joshua passed away, as soon as I knew they were both gone, I walked into Eric's hospital room. Tat boy was alive, and no one was there with him. Can't keep hold of a dead man's hand.

> *(**MIRI** and **RUTH** are still scrubbing their corner of the stage. In this scene **MIRI** is fifteen and **RUTH** is eight.)*

RUTH. *(To **MIRI**, seriously.)* Of course I want to have children. I think that's the best thing I could do one day – be a mother. But, I don't think I could handle more than six. What a headache.

MIRI. Six?

RUTH. Of course the number will be whatever God wants.

MIRI. You'd have to get married first, Ruth.

RUTH. *(Gravely.)* Yes. That will be hard. I love everyone.

MIRI. But who do you want to *kiss*, Ruth?

RUTH. Miri!

ABRAM. I'm happy to help you, if you need another pair of hands. I could ask Eli to come in the mornin's, and Aaron and I can come in the afternoons, if Samuel and John can't keep up. We can get it all done. That's how it's meant to be. You don't need that English man for the work.

JACOB. Forgiveness is hard, and with him here, I can't put it off. I need him for my work.

RUTH. I don't want to kiss anyone. I don't even want to think about kissin' anyone! *(Pause.)* Is that normal?

MIRI. One day you'll meet the right person, and you'll think about kissin' all the time.

RUTH. I don't know.

MIRI. You will. That's how it works. That's love.

RUTH. "And all who live in love, live in God."

MIRI. You'll see. When the bishop talks about the riches of heaven, all he means is love. It's not like there's piles of money up there. *(Pause.)* God is kissin'.

RUTH. *(Blushing.)* Miri! It's easy for you to say. You're goin' to marry Abram.

MIRI. If that's what God wants.

RUTH. It's surely what Abram wants.

MIRI. Well. Abram shouldn't get everythin' he wants. Just because he's a boy.

ABRAM. I don't think he's goin' to do well here. I hope he finds what he's lookin' for, but I don't think it's here. You can smell it on him. He's lost. He's wild. It's not your place to save people, Jacob, especially people who put us all in danger.

JACOB. Won't turn him out. We've already lost too much.

(**ABRAM** *tips his hat respectfully to* **JACOB** *and exits.* **JACOB** *begins shoveling again. After a moment,* **ERIC** *returns. He doesn't pick up his shovel, he just watches.*)

RUTH. You look worried.

MIRI. Just bored.

RUTH. Why? It's a beautiful day.

MIRI. Don't you ever just get bored?

RUTH. No, I love it.

MIRI. What? Scrubbin'?

RUTH. The whole world. And scrubbin'. *(Pause.)* Are you feelin' well?

MIRI. I heard from Elizabeth that when she went to Brooklyn on her *Rumspringa*, she saw a community garden. Where everyone had just a little spot and they came every day and tended just their little spot. All kinds of people. Black people, too. And Spanish people. All sharin' a garden in the city.

RUTH. How do they grow enough to eat if they only have a little spot?

MIRI. They mostly buy their food. The gardenin' is just for fun.

RUTH. Well, gardenin' *is* fun. But I don't know if I could do that. Be so close to lots of people, in a garden. In a city. I like the idea of it. It's nice. But it's too much. Too much happenin'. It wonders me. How could I deal with so many people?

MIRI. Maybe there are only a few people here, so everyone means too much to you.

RUTH. Maybe.

MIRI. *(Watching* **RUTH.***)* How can you love scrubbin'?

RUTH. It's so easy! And everythin' looks so clean after. Makes me feel proud. Like laundry. I love doin' laundry. It smells so good and it's so warm right off the line.

MIRI. I miss goin' to school. *(Pause.)* And I'm bad at foldin' sheets.

RUTH. It's just practice. I like it. It's comfortin'.

MIRI. You should practice bein' around strangers.

RUTH. I just like bein' around the house.

MIRI. That's okay. That's fine. *(Short pause.)* I'm jealous you're so content. I know that's a sin.

> *(They scrub in silence for a moment. Something occurs to **RUTH** and she stops her work for the first time.)*

RUTH. You're goin' to be baptized, aren't you? After your *Rumspringa*?

MIRI. When other people get baptized...I don't feel like I feel the way I should feel.

> *(**ERIC** has been watching **JACOB** shovel this whole time without helping. Now he interrupts the work.)*

ERIC. Are you in trouble?

JACOB. *(Realizing **ERIC** is there.)* What do you mean by tat?

RUTH. What are you sayin' now?

MIRI. I don't know. I'm just thinkin'.

RUTH. That's good.

MIRI. Sometimes it doesn't feel so good.

> *(**RUTH** and **MIRI** exit.)*

> *(**ESTHER** crosses from the kitchen to the porch, where she sits and begins patching a shirt.)*

ERIC. That...Abram...guy. Did he come here because you're in trouble? For having me on your farm?

JACOB. No. Abram came to check on us, because he's our neighbor. Because he cares about our family.

ERIC. But I –

JACOB. *(Gently.)* Do you always believe tat everythin' is about you?

ERIC. I'm sorry.

(**JACOB** *stops shoveling.*)

JACOB. You have said "I'm sorry" a lot this week. More than you have said anything else.

ERIC. I...yeah. I guess so.

JACOB. How many people have you apologized to in your life?

(**ERIC** *says nothing.*)

Apologies are just words, Eric. A man is not what he says. A man is what he does.

ERIC. Well, maybe "I'm sorry" is all I've got.

JACOB. I don't believe tat.

(**JACOB** *stares at* **ERIC** *for a moment.*)

(**JACOB** *hands* **ERIC** *a shovel and exits to the porch. He sits with* **ESTHER.**)

(*Silence.*)

(**JACOB** *watches* **ERIC** *shovel from the porch. After a moment,* **ERIC** *picks up both shovels and exits.*)

People tell me I talk too quietly.

ESTHER. You don't.

JACOB. People tell me I repeat myself.

ESTHER. You do.

JACOB. Think there's too much noise in te world. Was there this much noise when we were young? (*Pause.*) My parents didn't have a phone. Now we have a phone, at te end of te lane. It's sad. Not phones, not themselves, just needin' a phone is sad. Do we need it?

ESTHER. We decided we need it. To call a taxi. To call a doctor, if there's an emergency.

JACOB. (*Spiraling.*) There was an emergency, and te phone didn't help us. Did no good. (*Short pause.*) What I want is for us to be healthy and safe. I want everyone I know to go to heaven. Maybe I shouldn't want anythin'. Maybe I should trust God more. I regret that I haven't trusted Him more... (*Short pause.*) I don't help you enough. Could help with te washin'; don't care what te other men would think. Could be kinder with my remarks. Abram came by earlier and I was not as kind as I could've been. Was just offerin' us more help.

ESTHER. *(Looking up from her work.)* Jacob –

JACOB. *(Still casting around for a solution.)* Was never tested when I was young. That's why my faith is bein' tested now, now tat I'm old...

ESTHER. *(Placing her hand gently on his.)* There is nothin' you could have done. There is no way you could live tat would have prevented te accident.

JACOB. What did I owe God tat he needed so much repayment?

(Resolved.) I will not have any regrets about te English man.

> *(ERIC enters. ESTHER pulls her hand away from JACOB and blushes. ERIC is dressed in ill-fitting Amish clothes – a collared white shirt that is too large/small and black pants that are too short/long on him. He wears his English sneakers. It is shocking. And kind of funny.)*

Good evenin', Eric.

ERIC. Good evening, Jacob. Esther.

ESTHER. *(Quietly.)* Where...where did you get those?

ERIC. I...I found them. I know it's kind of...but I didn't bring a bag, and I've been wearing the same clothes since I got here...they really smell.

JACOB. Of course. You've been working very hard.

ERIC. Thank you...um, thanks. You... *(No...)* I like being here and... *(No...)* Actually, I was wondering, if it's not too much trouble? Could I give you these?

> *(ERIC holds out a very fancy cell phone, watch, and wallet to JACOB.)*

Would you take these from me? They're getting in my way. I think I'll work better without them.

JACOB. I think you're right. I'll put these in the house.

> (**JACOB** *exits into the house.*)

ESTHER. *(Evenly.)* Eric, you have been a very big help to us this week, and we're glad to have you here as long as you need to stay with us, but there's no need for you to dress this way. It's not quite appropriate. And your watch, your things...they look very valuable. I'm not sure we should –

> (**JACOB** *re-enters excitedly, a folded shirt, pants, and suspenders in his hands. He gives them to* **ERIC.**)

JACOB. *(Interrupting.)* I believe these will fit you better. Why don't you wear these instead?

> (**ESTHER** *looks at her husband with disapproval, but he continues.*)

Hard work is te way to salvation, Eric. Closest thing we have to God's will on earth. You have te right to hard work, and I hope tat these will help you.

ESTHER. *(Coolly.)* We'll put your other clothes in the wash.

ERIC. Thank you!

> (**RUTH** *enters with a jar of strawberry jam and a few spoons.*)

RUTH. I have such good news! The Yoders sent over some strawberry jam today. Would anybody like some? We have so much jam this evenin'! It's wonderful.

> (**ERIC** *is so excited to have the new Amish clothes that he forgets himself and begins to change into them right there on the porch. No one notices him at first, but when he drops his pants, the women gasp and turn their faces.*)

RUTH.	ESTHER.
Gracious!	Good heavenly days!

JACOB. Eric, perhaps you could –

(The commotion is interrupted abruptly: **MIRI** *enters, dressed in modern English clothes, wheeling a small suitcase behind her. Total silence descends. No one speaks, no one moves for an uncomfortable period of time.* **ERIC** *looks around, a little confused but not wanting to make a move. Finally,* **RUTH** *breaks the spell. She runs over to* **MIRI,** *still with the jam jar and spoons in her hands, and wraps* **MIRI** *in a suffocating hug.)*

RUTH. *(To* **MIRI.***)* You're home! You're home, and we have so much strawberry jam!

(Lights dim on the porch. There is a sound and light cue to indicate transition into the next movement.)

Scene Three: Waste

(The Past.)

(Lights up on the living room. **JACOB** *is sitting, frozen. It is five years in the past.* **ESTHER** *enters from the porch, in a hurry.)*

ESTHER. We're goin' to be late.

JACOB. Can't make myself move.

ESTHER. Of course you can. You must. He's doin' this for her.

JACOB. He's not.

ESTHER. Can't be late for worship again. Last time te bishop's wife nearly cut me in two with her eyes.

JACOB. Are we really all just goin' to sit there and listen to him talk about it?

ESTHER. He needs to confess. He needs to be heard. *(Pause.)* Miri should think about doin' tat for herself.

JACOB. It wasn't her doin'.

ESTHER. I'm not sayin' it was. But she's always where she's not supposed to be. Always doin' what we tell her not to do.

JACOB. No. I can't hear it. Can't go.

> *(***ESTHER** *fixes her eyes on* **JACOB**.*)*

ESTHER. Get your hat, and get in te buggy. It's time.

> *(***ESTHER** *exits to the porch.* **JACOB** *doesn't follow her.)*
>
> *(Shift -> The Present.)*
>
> *(As indicated by a sound and light cue.)*
>
> *(***MIRI** *and* **ERIC** *are in the barn.)*
>
> *(***ERIC** *is finishing putting on his better-fitting Amish clothes. They have not been introduced.)*

ERIC. Do you want the hayloft? Or to sleep down here? I've been sleeping in the loft; it's cooler up there. I've just been sweating a lot since I got here. But then I wake up in the middle of the night and I'm freezing. So I have all the blankets up there. But I can bring some down.

MIRI. You talk a lot.

ERIC. I'm Eric.

MIRI. Good for you.

ERIC. It's warmer down here, closer to the animals.

MIRI. Getting a tour from a fucking tourist. *(Pause.)* You look ridiculous, you know that?

ERIC. It's a... *(No...)* I want to –

MIRI. Gross.

ERIC. What?

MIRI. You! This whole thing.

ERIC. You don't even know me.

MIRI. You're right. What are you into, farming? Woodworking? Construction? People come through here to rip off all kinds of things.

ERIC. I'm not ripping anything off. I just need to be here.

MIRI. Right. There's nothing in it for you. You were just real super interested in the Amish, and it didn't occur to you that they don't owe you anything.

ERIC. I'm on... I'm on a journey right now. Jacob is helping me work through some hard stuff here.

MIRI. *(Interrupting.)* This family is grieving, did you know that?

ERIC. I'm grieving, too. *(Pause.)* I wouldn't be here, if I had anywhere else to be.

MIRI. *(Pause.)* I'll sleep down here.

ERIC. There are blankets in the hayloft.

MIRI. I know where the goddamn blankets are, Jesus!

ERIC. *(Fuming.)* I'm going to go check on Honey.

(**ERIC** *exits.*)

MIRI. Who the fuck is Honey?

(**RUTH** *enters with a glass of milk.*)

This is bullshit!

RUTH. Your words! Please, Miri.

MIRI. *(Seeing her.)* Sorry. This is *ridiculous*. I have to sleep in the barn.

RUTH. Well surely you didn't think they were goin' to let you sleep in the house?

MIRI. I don't know what I expected.

RUTH. You should've come in the mornin', not the evenin'.

MIRI. I didn't think about the time. When I got your letter, I just threw a bunch of stuff into my suitcase and left.

RUTH. If you want...there's one of your old dresses in the house, and I have an extra coverin', if –

MIRI. No.

RUTH. Some ex-Amish do, you know. Dress Amish when they visit.

MIRI. That's hypocritical.

RUTH. Give them a little somethin'. A little comfort.

MIRI. They won't even let me sleep in the house!

RUTH. I know. But maybe soon?

MIRI. I have to sleep in the *barn*. Like an animal. Like that English...who is he, exactly?

RUTH. *(Carefully.)* He's Eric. He's helpin' out on the farm.

MIRI. Like an internship or something?

RUTH. He's the driver. The English that hit our buggy.

   (Silence.)

MIRI. *(In shock.)* He killed Levi and Joshua?

RUTH. He's lost his way. He needs us.

MIRI. I don't give a fuck what *he* needs!

RUTH. Words!

MIRI. I'm sorry! I'm sorry, Ruth! But the man that killed our brothers is sleeping in this barn!

RUTH. It helps Dat to have Eric around.

MIRI. What? Why?

RUTH. I don't really know. But please don't come start a big fight, okay? You just got back. He's a nice man. He doesn't cause trouble.

MIRI. *(Hostile.)* But I do?

RUTH. You're puttin' words in my mouth. And right now, I'm the only one who wants you here!

> *(Beat.)*

MIRI. I thought, with the boys gone... I thought they might need me to be here.

RUTH. They'll come around.

MIRI. It's good to see you, Ruth.

RUTH. It's good to see you, too. I miss you so much. I brought you a glass of milk.

> (**RUTH** *puts the glass of milk on the ground. She is not allowed to touch her excommunicated sister, give her anything, or take anything from her hand. The hug in the last scene was involuntary, but* **RUTH** *has control of herself again.)*

MIRI. I don't want a glass of milk, thank you.

RUTH. You can take it to Eric.

MIRI. I will not.

RUTH. Then I'll take it to him.

> (**RUTH** *hugs* **MIRI.** **ERIC** *re-enters.)*

Things will be better in the mornin'. You'll see.

> (**MIRI** *exits.* **RUTH** *walks over to* **ERIC.** **ABRAM** *enters and watches as* **RUTH** *gives* **ERIC** *the glass of milk and he drinks it.* **RUTH** *smiles at* **ERIC** *and* **ERIC** *smiles at* **RUTH.** **RUTH** *does not see* **ABRAM.** *She exits.)*
>
> *(It is now daytime.)*

ABRAM. *(To* **ERIC.***)* I know why you're here.

ERIC. Do you? I don't.

ABRAM. You can't make this right by doin' chores, even if you could do the work of four men. Even if you could do the work of one man.

> (**ERIC** *says nothing.)*

There's no amount of manure you can shovel or peaches you can put up or acres you can plow that will even the score.

(**ERIC** *says nothing.*)

(*Pause.*) I've seen the way you look at our women.

ERIC. Come on, dude, *your* women?

ABRAM. You have ideas about our women. All you English do. You think they're unspoilt, and hard-workin', and angelic. They are. You can't have one.

ERIC. With charm like that, I don't know why you're threatened by me.

ABRAM. I've seen you with Ruth.

ERIC. Ruth is kind to me. And she lets me be kind to her.

ABRAM. Ruth is taken care of. She doesn't need you. The less you see of her, the better for everyone.

ERIC. What's your problem? I haven't done anything to you.

ABRAM. See, that's why you don't belong here. You don't understand community. You took two young men from us, men who were almost brothers to me. It's not just Jacob and Esther and Ruth you took from.

ERIC. I know about community, okay? I grew up in a very nice cul-de-sac.

ABRAM. This family is bein' kind, because it's not our way to turn out pitiful souls in search of refuge. But you've been makin' *more* work around here, for days. They don't want you here any more than I do.

(**ERIC** *exits with the glass.* **MIRI** *enters.* **ABRAM** *looks at* **MIRI***. They are now in front of the convenience store.*)

(*To* **MIRI**.) It's been a long time since you've been here. And you don't live here.

MIRI. Abram.

ABRAM. It's very nice to see you again, but you don't live here. I do.

MIRI. I don't live here *because* you do.

ABRAM. That's hurtful.

MIRI. I don't know what you want from me.

ABRAM. Nothin'. I want nothin' from you. No one here wants anythin' from you. We're all doin' just fine.

MIRI. My family needs me.

ABRAM. They're not your family anymore.

MIRI. This is bigger than your stupid laws. It's outside the *Ordnung.*

ABRAM. The *Ordnung* is from God. And all of this, their grief, is part of God's plan.

MIRI. And do you think it was God's plan that I left? God's plan that I lost my whole life over something *you* did?

ABRAM. *(Deflecting.)* I don't speak for God.

> *(MIRI approaches ABRAM and roughly touches his clean-shaven chin.)*

MIRI. You never got married. Was that God's plan? Or yours?

> *(ABRAM pulls away from her. RUTH enters.)*

RUTH. *(Brightly.)* Hello.

ABRAM. Ruth, would you like to go walkin'?

RUTH. A walk? With me?

ABRAM. Let me walk you to the Yoders' farm.

RUTH. Oh. Okay. Thank you.

MIRI. What is this?

ABRAM. So nice to see you, Miri.

> *(ABRAM exits with RUTH. MIRI watches them leave. ERIC enters; she doesn't see him.)*

ERIC. I think they have a crush on each other.

MIRI. *(Whirling around.)* What? Oh. You. No. That's not possible. He was just trying to get away from me.

ERIC. He comes around a lot. I think he wants to see your sister.

MIRI. You don't know what you're talking about. Trust me.

ERIC. Who wouldn't want to be with that dude? He's like, the LeBron James of being Amish.

MIRI. He's just playing a game.

ERIC. I mean, I personally think he's a piece of shit. But I've heard all these amazing things about how good he is at like, building barns and shoeing horses and stuff. He sounds amazing. His shoulders are also amazing. But I guess he can't grow a beard, so...

MIRI. Only married Amish wear beards.

ERIC. Oh. So he's not making, like, a rebellious fashion choice?

MIRI. You don't know anything about anything.

ERIC. Actually, I don't know anything about pretty much everything.

MIRI. You think you're clever? You want to have a little chat? Awesome. Why don't you tell me, straight up, what you're doing here? Did you lose your job? Lose your apartment? You must really be hard up if your best move right now is to camp out in the family barn of the two people you fucking murdered. Levi was twenty-three. Joshua was twenty.

ERIC. I know. I'm sor– *(No...)* I know.

MIRI. Not good enough.

ERIC. I'm working on a more authentic way to make amends.

MIRI. I want you out of here!

ERIC. *(Short pause.)* Respectfully, Miri? You can't make me go.

MIRI. You're a really shitty person.

ERIC. I am. Yeah. But this part, right now? This is not the shitty part.

> *(Beat. She turns to leave.)*

You know, your dad reminds me of my dad. But he like...means it.

> *(**MIRI** turns back to him but says nothing.)*

My family is Catholic. There's a lot of really good parts, but no one ever tries to like, *live* them. And it just pisses me off, you know, to sit in the middle of all this bullshit, knowing that everyone knows the right thing, but doesn't do it. It's not like that here. They make everyone live the good parts.

(Pause.) I was sure I didn't believe in anything anymore, two weeks ago. But being here, I realize that it's not God I have the problem with. It's his fucking followers.

(Beat.)

MIRI. Tell me about the accident.

ERIC. I don't think... *(No...)* I'm probably not...

MIRI. *(Interrupting.)* You want to authentically make amends with me? Tell me about that day. All of it.

> *(On a different part of the stage, unseen by* **ERIC** *and* **MIRI**, **ESTHER** *enters and begins to throw eggs, as hard as she can, against the side of the barn. She is silent at first, but her rage and the exertion of the task eventually lead to loud grunting/crying noises.)*

> (**ESTHER** *can't see/hear the others, and they can't see/hear her.)*

ERIC. *(Pause.)* I drink. A lot. Alone. I mean, I'm quitting. I quit. I haven't had a drink since. *(No...)* I was on about day four of a bender and I was just not disappearing the way I usually could. There was still so much of me around. I got into my car. Just to drive... *(No...)* just to outrun...the thing. I was driving for a long time. Not speeding. Not being reckless. Hours. I had a full tank when I started. I wasn't really drunk then, at that point, but I hadn't slept in days. It was about 6:30. The sun was going down. I was running out of gas. I thought to myself, "Well, you'll just run out of gas, and maybe you'll just pull over on the side of the road and stay there. What would you be going back to if you turned around?" I was close to here. I didn't know the place, but the sun was so nice. Nice colors. It's really hypnotic to drive, around here. The hills and the fields and... *(No...)* I didn't feel happy right then, but I felt nothing. Finally. My head was getting light. Lifting off like a balloon. I felt myself fall asleep, and it felt so nice, and I really didn't care if I never woke up again. I drifted, then my whole body exploded. I opened my eyes in a turned-over car. And I thought, "You did it. You're dead." I didn't know that anyone else was involved until I woke up in the hospital the next day. *(Pause.)* They were just trying to get home before dark.

(**MIRI** *says nothing.*)

(**ESTHER** *has run out of eggs. She looks exhausted. She pants.*)

I wasn't legally drunk when I ran up on the buggy. Just tired. Legally, it was an accident, even though it was completely my fault. Your parents won't press charges. That's why I came here, actually. I asked them to. And they forgave me instead.

(**MIRI** *says nothing.*)

(**ESTHER** *hears someone coming. Embarrassed and ashamed,* **ESTHER** *exits.* **JACOB** *enters and sees the mess she left.*)

So I know they can forgive you. Whatever you did.

MIRI. What *I* did?! Me?

ERIC. Even if you're shunned.

(**JACOB** *takes in the destruction for a moment longer, then exits the way he came.*)

MIRI. I'm not shunned. Shunning is temporary. Shunning is for people you still believe in. I'm excommunicated. I don't exist.

(Refocusing on **ERIC.***)* YOU should be in jail.

ERIC. I should be. But I'm forgiven.

MIRI. Oh no. No. Forgiveness is a trick.

ERIC. All the problems of the world could be solved if everyone forgave each other the way your parents forgave me.

MIRI. Could you fetishize them any more? Forgiveness is a shortcut, to get around things that are messy. It's imaginary higher ground to retreat to, for people who are too scared to fight.

ERIC. You don't believe in forgiveness?

MIRI. No. And you shouldn't either. *(Short pause.)* This is not going to happen again.

> *(**RUTH** enters the kitchen and begins setting the table for dinner.)*
>
> *(**ESTHER** and **JACOB** enter. A place is set for **MIRI**, and one for **ERIC**. Then the three of them take their places at the table.)*
>
> *(**ERIC** sits down at the table. **MIRI** turns to her family.)*

(Sees the table.) I want to eat supper.

ESTHER. Ruth put a plate on te porch for you.

MIRI. I want to sit at the table.

ESTHER. You know you can't.

MIRI. *(Pointing.)* There! There's my place.

ESTHER. Miri, please.

MIRI. You let this *stranger* get away with *murder*, but you won't let me get away with leaving?

JACOB. *(Angered, loudly.)* MIRIAM! There is supper for you on te porch!

> *(**MIRI** crosses to the porch. **JACOB**, **ESTHER**, **RUTH**, and **ERIC** take their plates and exit. **ABRAM** enters. It is now later that evening.)*

ABRAM. Good evening, Miri.

MIRI. Go home.

ABRAM. Come to talk to your dat.

MIRI. I should have *killed* you five years ago. And if you touch Ruth. If you even breathe in her direction. I will do it now.

ABRAM. *(Coolly.)* You aren't better than me. You aren't smarter than me. *(Pause.)* I don't believe you.

> *(**MIRI** begins to leave in a fury and **RUTH** enters at her back. **RUTH** approaches **ABRAM**, but **MIRI** does not see her. **ERIC** enters, crossing to **MIRI**. He is holding an Amish dress.)*

ERIC. I found this on the clothesline.

MIRI. And?

ERIC. *(Sincerely trying to help.)* And I thought it might help. If you wore it. And if you weren't so mean. It might help things.

> (**MIRI** *snatches the dress from him and exits.* **ERIC** *exits after her.)*
>
> *(Lights dim.)*
>
> *(There is a sound and light cue to indicate transition into the next movement.)*

Scene Four: Touch

(The Present.)

(**ABRAM** *and* **RUTH** *are walking. It is not a sweet walk, it is uncomfortable and forced-feeling, with lots of heavy pauses.)*

ABRAM. Did you get all your chores done?

RUTH. Yes. For the mornin'.

(A short silence.)

Did you...get...all your chores done?

ABRAM. *(Chuckling good-naturedly.)* Yes.

(A short silence.)

It's a beautiful day.

RUTH. Yes! Such a blue sky.

ABRAM. Yes. I got up very early, and the air was so nice and cool I knew it would be a good day to ask you for a walk.

RUTH. *(Excited, what a thing to have in common!)* I got up very early, too!

(A short silence.)

(Calmer.) There is more laundry now with Eric here. Not as much as there...once was, but –

ABRAM. *(Interrupting.)* You're doin' his laundry?

RUTH. I don't mind! I put it in with ours. He's helping Dat so much. And I love the smell of clean laundry. I don't mind more of that.

ABRAM. How long do you think the English will stay?

RUTH. His name is Eric, you know that. His comin' to us was God's doin'. Eric is a person who needs help.

ABRAM. Everythin' seems to be too much for him.

RUTH. It's nice havin' new people around.

ABRAM. He's a weak man. I've been prayin' for him. Since the first time I saw him. Everyone knows you shovel with your legs and shoulders, but there he was, shovelin' away with his little wrists.

(A short silence.)

Do you forgive Eric?

RUTH. *(Nodding.)* Uh-huh. He's a good person, I think. And he's not so lost anymore. His hands don't shake. He sits still at the table. He speaks more slowly.

ABRAM. You give farm work the credit for that?

RUTH. I give God the credit.

(A short silence.)

ABRAM. I heard you have a new horse?

RUTH. Yes! Dat named her Honey. She's my new favorite. She's very sweet. And young.

ABRAM. Good. *(Pause.)* Are you enjoyin' our walk?

RUTH. The day is lovely.

(A short silence.)

ABRAM. Am I borin' you?

RUTH. No! My goodness! I feel like I'm borin' you.

ABRAM. I think my stories are interestin', to me.

RUTH. *(Overlapping.)* I think mine are interestin', too.

ABRAM. *(Overlapping.)* But sometimes I'm tellin' a story to someone and then I look into his eyes and the look there says, "Is this over?"

RUTH. I like your stories, Abram.

(A short silence.)

ABRAM. Were you surprised that Miri came back?

RUTH. No. *(Pause.)* I wrote to her. All along. When she left I felt like I lost my right arm.

(A short silence.)

ABRAM. Would you like to go on another walk with me soon?

RUTH. I do like to walk.

ABRAM. Is that a yes?

> (**ERIC** *approaches the porch with* **JACOB**, *deep in conversation at the end of a hard day's work.*)

JACOB. Yes.

> (**RUTH** *smiles at* **ABRAM** *politely, then exits.*)

ABRAM. Ruth? Is that a yes?

> (**ABRAM** *exits after* **RUTH.**)

JACOB. Yes. "The Lord God took the man and put him into the Garden of Eden to dress it and to keep it." Treat people well and do your work – it's all you can do in this life. Now, it would be prideful to think tat just because we are Amish, we're all goin' to heaven. We don't think tat way. We do work, and we do hope.

ERIC. I like the repetitive, physical stuff. I like sleeping in the barn. I like living in my body, instead of my head. I like going to sleep exhausted. And, AND, it's been two weeks since I got here and I don't even think about drinking anymore. You should be charging me for this. Really. I've been to lots of expensive rehab places that weren't half this effective.

JACOB. Two weeks seems too fast.

ERIC. It does, but I really don't want a drink, not at all. I do good work, and I can put my hands on it. I can be in the same room as myself now, and not need a distraction. It's like I've been staring down a long tunnel, at just one thing, but suddenly the tunnel is gone, and I'm looking around me for the first time in years.

JACOB. Eric, you work very hard. We are glad to have you here. But you came to us, just two weeks ago, with a burden. If that burden is still inside you, you can't ignore it. Just be substitutin' one thing for another.

ERIC. You think I'm substituting being Amish for drinking?

JACOB. No. You are not Amish, Eric.

ERIC. I know. I know. But before now, my whole life was just want, get, use, repeat – day after day after day. I can see the bigger picture now. This life is a real blessing. Maybe the first one I've ever had.

JACOB. You've had many blessin's. Of tat I'm sure.

ERIC. *(Getting worked up.)* Things are simple here. It's better. Rules mean something, because people actually care about them.

JACOB. This is all new to you. But it's just life. It's work, it's family. There's no magic here.

ERIC. *(Almost frantic.)* And the whole issue of what it means to be a man! Ha! Don't even get me started. I look at myself, and I'm just so *weak*. But I look at you and Abram and the others, and I think of your sons – MEN. I'm going to do that. I'm going to be like that. The work will make me into a man. I might lose all my hair one day, I mean, I probably will lose all my hair, that's hereditary, but I'll have SHOULDERS. I won't be a coward. Not anymore. I won't be so afraid to fail that I don't even try. Not anymore. Not now that I know how to do it right, when everyone out there, everyone I used to know, is doing it wrong.

JACOB. *(Irritated.)* Takin' our beliefs and usin' them as judgments against other people is not te point.

> *(Beat.)*

ERIC. I've been to the top of Machu Picchu. I've been to temples in Thailand. I went to Catholic school for ten years. And I feel closer to God sleeping in your barn than I ever have, anywhere else.

> *(JACOB considers this.)*

JACOB. *(Pause.)* Would you like to learn to drive te buggy?

ERIC. YES!

JACOB. I recommend drivin' a horse and buggy for a lot of reasons. Very peaceful. Slow. Relaxin', if you don't have anywhere to be. People do very funny things as we go by. It's a good time for thinkin'.

ERIC. Can we do that now?

JACOB. No. Tomorrow. After we plow te back field, I think. Perhaps Ruth can come with us.

ERIC. And Miri?

(*JACOB seems to be about to respond in the affirmative, but he sees ESTHER enter.*)

JACOB. *(Pause.)* We should just go alone.

ESTHER. Tat's for te best.

ERIC. Okay. Tomorrow!

(**ERIC** *exits, excited.* **JACOB** *does not cross to* **ESTHER**. *There is a gulf between them.*)

ESTHER. You're the head of this family. You must tell her to leave.

JACOB. She's only been here a few days. Not too long.

ESTHER. Too long.

JACOB. She sleeps in te barn. She takes her meals on te porch. She helps Ruth with te laundry.

ESTHER. She won't even dress appropriately. She's goin' to hell. She isn't our daughter.

JACOB. I cannot.

ESTHER. People are talkin'. Startin' to talk.

JACOB. Let them talk. Our daughter came here for comfort.

ESTHER. We are not allowed to touch her.

JACOB. We need comfort as well. How can we give it to Eric and not our own flesh and blood?

ESTHER. It would be different if she'd never been baptized, if she'd left before, but she *was* baptized. And she broke tat vow.

JACOB. You're tellin' me to force her to leave?

ESTHER. You're my husband, and te head of this house. I'll follow where you lead. But try to think about it from my place. I'm blamed for raisin' her. I don't want to be shut out. Not now. Not when we need our neighbors and our friends.

(**ESTHER** *makes a decision. She is going to tell her most painful family story, not to elicit pity, but to illustrate what happens when death is not dealt with properly, according to the Amish way. It is a tactic to get what* *she wants from her husband, which is not comfort, but resolve.)*

My mother was different from te other women. Didn't get along with anybody. She wasn't part of te community. I don't think she really wanted to be a mother. *(Pause.)* I was sixteen when it happened. We were all goin' swimmin' down at te small lake, and she went first, to set up lunch. And by te time we arrived, she had already drowned. My father was furious. At her, at us, at God. He shouldn't have been, but he was. Why is there so much anger all te time? His anger made it harder for us to go on, after. Miri's anger is makin' it harder for us to go on, now.

> *(MIRI enters at a different part of the stage. We see her contemplating the Amish dress and head covering in her hand. Very slowly, we see her take off her English clothes and put on the dress and covering. She leaves on her English shoes.)*

Since she came back here, it's harder for me to mourn Levi and Joshua. Harder to let go. She has tat anger, my family's anger. She resents us for our choices. Makes it harder to follow God's will.

JACOB. You are talkin' about your *daughter*!

> *(MIRI takes off her English shoes and is barefoot.)*

ESTHER. *(Raising her voice.)* I mourned so much when she left, even if you never saw tat! But she can't come and go in and out of our lives as she pleases.

JACOB. *(Angrily.)* We had four children, and now you tell me I have one! One! No. I won't ask Miri to leave. Not after five years of constant worryin', blamin' myself. No.

ESTHER. She is no more our daughter than tat English is our son! You can't bring them back. Not Miri, and not te boys. Givin' him their clothes, their chores, it's all just pastin' over. Levi and Joshua are dead.

JACOB. As if I did not know tat! They're gone. It's a tragedy.
An accident. But their sister comes back, and we turn
her away? Tat shames us.

> (*A short silence.* **MIRI** *exits with her English
> clothes and shoes in hand.*)

ESTHER. (*Slowly.*) She isn't back for good, you know. Never
asked to stay. Won't even cover her head. She still hates
this place, won't submit to the *Ordnung*. She's only here
until she feels better, and then she'll leave again. And
you'll never hear from her again. And te English will
leave, too. When our life gets too hard or too boring for
him. You can't keep them.

JACOB. You are a frightenin' woman. Like your mother.

> (**ESTHER** *nods.* **MIRI** *enters in her Amish
> plainclothes for the first time in the present.
> She is carrying a basket of eggs. Her parents
> register this change.*)

MIRI. I got the eggs, Dat. There were only a few in the laying
boxes.

JACOB. (*Collecting himself.*) That's very kind of you, Miri.
Thank you.

> (**MIRI** *starts to give the basket to* **JACOB** *but he
> cannot take it. He can't take anything out of
> her hand. She remembers this after a second
> and puts the basket on the ground.* **JACOB**
> *picks it up.*)

MIRI. The side of the barn is covered in broken eggs. Have
you seen it?

> (**ESTHER** *coughs loudly, surprised.*)

JACOB. Yes. Noticed tat.

MIRI. What could make such a mess?

ESTHER. Te chickens. They run around.

MIRI. The chickens?

ESTHER. They run around. Sometimes they kick eggs. They
kick them.

MIRI. Some of those eggshells are up *really* high.

ESTHER. They run around.

JACOB. I think we all agree tat te chickens run around.

MIRI. I can clean it up, if you need me to.

JACOB. No, you won't clean it up.

MIRI. I'll ask Ruth to help me. I really don't mind.

JACOB. Haven't sorted out who's goin' to clean tat yet.

ESTHER. *(Quickly.)* I'll take care of it.

JACOB. Then it's settled.

MIRI. Okay. Fine.

JACOB. It's a lot of wasted eggs.

ESTHER. I know.

(**ESTHER** *exits.*)

MIRI. I guess you can't teach chickens self-control.

JACOB. Nor obedience. Nor takin' responsibility for their lapses. Nor respect for their elders.

MIRI. Dat...

JACOB. But those things are hard for everyone, not just stupid chickens.

MIRI. Yes.

(*A beat between them.*)

JACOB. Miri-girl, are you plannin' to stay?

MIRI. You mean, forever? Be Amish again?

JACOB. Yes. You could. The Stoltzfus's oldest was gone nine years and came back. Made confession. Married an Amish girl.

MIRI. No, Dat. I'm not going to stay. You know that.

JACOB. What happened to you, was so long ago –

MIRI. *(Bitterly.)* I'm glad *you* feel that way.

JACOB. I don't mean to hurt you by sayin' tat. I just meant – perhaps you've made your point.

MIRI. You think I left as, what, some kind of stunt? To get attention?

JACOB. What more could we have done for you?

MIRI. You could have stood next to me. When he confessed. You could have held my hand.

JACOB. On te women's side?

MIRI. Yes. You, and Joshua, and Levi. You could have crossed the aisle and stood with me on the women's side of the congregation, just for that day. Just for that moment, when I really needed you.

JACOB. You've been gone a long time. You don't remember how it is.

MIRI. Oh, I do. I do remember. And that's why I wish, so desperately, that you'd had the balls to say, "Fuck the bishop, fuck the bishop's wife, and all the deacons, and all these judgmental assholes, I'm going to go stand on the other side, where my daughter *needs* me. Just for one day, *that's* going to be more important."

(*A beat between them.* **JACOB** *bristles.*)

JACOB. (*Evenly.*) We're all goin' through a lot right now. But it doesn't give you te right to talk to your father tat way. Like a spoilt English girl. Won't listen to it.

MIRI. (*Softening.*) Dat, please don't be angry.

JACOB. Not angry. Everythin' is wonderful.

(**JACOB** *exits with the eggs.* **MIRI** *exits the opposite way.* **ERIC** *and* **RUTH** *enter at a different part of the stage, on the porch.*)

RUTH. It's part of the *Ordnung*. It's how we do forgiveness. For big stuff.

ERIC. Everything is totally forgotten? Like it never happened?

RUTH. That's the idea. Like nothin' ever happened. Speak, forgive, forget. We go before the whole community and confess our big mistake. Then everyone decides whether or not to forgive. Or...they deliberate a while. But then they always forgive. And after that, the sin is absolved, and we never speak of it again. No one is allowed to hold it against the sinner anymore.

ERIC. A totally clean slate. No resentments. No gossip.

RUTH. Can't gossip.

ERIC. Oh! Maybe I could do that! I could go before everyone and confess.

RUTH. *(Delicately.)* Eric...you aren't Amish.

> (**MIRI** *and* **ABRAM** *enter, in the past. He is covering her eyes with his hands and leading her onstage. He is carrying a basket and she carries a lantern.)*

ABRAM. Just a little bit farther.

MIRI. *(Eyes covered.)* Where are we going?

ERIC. But I want forgiveness.

RUTH. You have our forgiveness.

ABRAM. We're almost there.

ERIC. Yeah, you all say that, but I don't feel it. It's too easy. I want to do something hard, so I can feel like I really earned it.

RUTH. Forgiveness isn't a thing that can be earned, Eric. You can't deserve it more one way or another. Either it's given, or it's not given.

> (**ERIC** *and* **RUTH** *exit.)*
>
> *(Shift -> The Past.)*
>
> *(As indicated by a sound and light cue.)*
>
> (**ABRAM** *and* **MIRI** *are deep in the woods somewhere; it is dusk. He uncovers her eyes.)*

MIRI. We're nowhere.

ABRAM. Exactly.

MIRI. Exactly what?

ABRAM. No one is here but us.

> (**ABRAM** *begins taking things out of the basket: a quilt, some biscuits, candy bars. He spreads the quilt on the ground and motions for* **MIRI** *to sit. Then* **ABRAM** *takes a bottle of wine out of the picnic basket.)*

MIRI. Where the hell did you get that?

ABRAM. The English gas station. They asked to see my ID and I told them I don't have one, I'm Amish. And they sold it to me anyway. Because I'm tall.

MIRI. You don't think we're goin' to drink that right now, do you?

ABRAM. Why not? It's your birthday.

MIRI. In a month.

ABRAM. We just got baptized.

MIRI. Great. Now we're Amish, let's get drunk?

ABRAM. Soon we'll be married.

MIRI. So you tell me.

ABRAM. I've talked to your dat about it.

MIRI. You know, you've never asked me if I want to marry you.

ABRAM. Well, I assumed if you didn't want to, you'd've said somethin' by now.

MIRI. You should still ask me. You shouldn't just assume.

ABRAM. *(Playfully, a nursery rhyme.)* Miri may I marry you?

MIRI. Be serious about it.

ABRAM. Oh fine. Miriam, would you do me the honor of bein' my wife, and livin' in my home, and raisin' my children, and buryin' me when I die?

MIRI. *(Pause.)* I will. I especially look forward to buryin' you.

ABRAM. See? That was unnecessary.

MIRI. No. It was nice.

> *(There is short, happy silence. They are both very pleased.)*

Do you think heaven is like havin' all the food you could ever want, OR, is it like never bein' hungry?

ABRAM. *(Pensive.)* I think all the food you want sounds better.

MIRI. I think so, too. But Dat says it's the other way around. That I'm bein' worldly. In heaven you don't have any needs or desires.

ABRAM. That can't be right. That's not paradise. That's boring.

MIRI. That's what I think. I'd rather have anything I want than not want anything.

ABRAM. Me, too.

> (*A short pause. Then* **ABRAM** *lunges at* **MIRI** *across the blanket.*)

MIRI. (*Shocked.*) What are you doin'?

ABRAM. I'm tryin' to kiss you.

MIRI. Tryin' to kill me.

> (**ABRAM** *rights himself, takes* **MIRI***'s face tenderly in his hands, and kisses her. This is their first kiss. It is awkward and tentative and lovely. It makes us ache.*)

ABRAM. That was nice.

MIRI. Kiss me again.

> (**ABRAM** *kisses* **MIRI** *again.*)

Yes. I think I could do that for forty or fifty years. If only you wouldn't talk so much in between.

> (**ABRAM** *kisses* **MIRI** *again, and this time it is passionate and she gives herself over to it. After a moment, he tries to lay her down on the quilt.*)

What are you doin'?

ABRAM. Be calm. I'll take care of you.

> (**MIRI** *tries to get out from under him but he is too strong for her.*)

You don't have to pretend to be good. This is me. I know you.

MIRI. I know you, too. This doesn't feel right.

ABRAM. You're goin' to be my wife. You said so.

MIRI. I'm not your wife. Not yet.

ABRAM. *(Forcefully.)* Stop fightin' me. You're always fightin' me.

> (**ABRAM** *wraps his large hand around* **MIRI***'s neck and holds her still.*)

MIRI. Abram?

> *(Zero-count blackout.)*

End of Act One

Intermission

[Handwritten notes:]
Miri raped by Abram?

Ruth is being courted by Abram.

Hard for Jacob & Esther to trust Miri.

ACT TWO

Scene Five: Ask

(The Past, seven years ago.)

(As indicated by sound and lights.)

(Lights up on **ABRAM** *and* **MIRI** *setting up for worship in a barn.)*

ABRAM. I have news. I'm goin' to buy a truck.

MIRI. A truck?! You're not.

ABRAM. In six months, when I start *Rumspringa*. I have almost enough saved for a cheap used one. English family up the road has that red one in their front yard they're tryin' to sell.

MIRI. A red truck! *(Pause.)* Could I sit in it?

ABRAM. When I imagine it, you're sittin' in it.

MIRI. I bet you like thinkin' of yourself in a truck.

ABRAM. I like thinkin' of us both in my truck.

MIRI. Would you drive me to town? To the library?

ABRAM. I would drive you to town, and I would pick you up.

MIRI. I'm goin' to get a library card when I start *Rumspringa*. And I'm goin' to wear English clothes when I go to town.

ABRAM. What else are you goin' to do?

MIRI. I don't know yet.

ABRAM. A library card and English clothes? That's *it*?

MIRI. I'm goin' to read all the books in the back room. The ones we're not allowed to see.

ABRAM. That's all you want to do?

MIRI. I don't know...maybe I'll cut my hair. And travel! Go to New Orleans. Or California. Wear an English bathin' suit on the beach.

ABRAM. *(Wide-eyed and serious.)* If you wear an English bathin' suit I will drive you to California to the beach.

MIRI. *(Laughing.)* You can't even drive, except for a buggy! You're goin' to spend all your savin's on a truck that you won't be able to even drive.

ABRAM. I'll take lessons. Can't be that hard. And then we can do whatever we want.

MIRI. Within reason.

ABRAM. It's *Rumspringa.* We can do WHATEVER we want.

MIRI. *(Pause.)* Why do I get the feelin' that you're talkin' about somethin' particular right now?

    (A short beat between them.)

ABRAM. I want to try cocaine.

MIRI. *(Horrified and surprised.)* WHAT?!

ABRAM. I want to try cocaine. With you. I want us to do it together.

MIRI. What even...what even is it? Abram, I don't know what it even is but I know it's very, very bad. What's wrong with you? People die from cocaine, don't they?

ABRAM. People don't die from cocaine! Don't be silly.

MIRI. How do you... Why do you want to know about this thing?

ABRAM. The English boys talk about it all the time. It sounds fun! I know where I can get some, from an English on this construction job I've been workin'.

MIRI. No.

ABRAM. No what?

MIRI. No, I won't do it.

ABRAM. But it won't be fun without you!

MIRI. I don't know anythin' about cocaine, except that it's bad.

ABRAM. If it's bad, I'll take care of you.

(**ABRAM** *takes* **MIRI**'*s hand. It's the first time anyone's ever touched her like this. She softens.*)

MIRI. We can't...we couldn't...hmm. Hmmm. We'd have to... Where would we put it?

ABRAM. In the truck! The truck solves all our problems!

MIRI. And...we couldn't eat...it. Here.

ABRAM. We could drive out somewhere and try it and stay there until it wears off, and sleep there, and then we could drive back.

MIRI. Sleep...?

MIRI & ABRAM. In the truck.

MIRI. Together?

ABRAM. Or I could sleep in the back.

MIRI. Maybe we...maybe we could try alcohol, first? And see how that goes?

ABRAM. (*Excited.*) Yes!

(**ABRAM** *picks up* **MIRI** *and twirls her around. He puts her down. They almost kiss, but don't.*)

Promise me one thing you won't do, on *Rumspringa*?

MIRI. What's that?

ABRAM. Don't move to town. Stay here with me.

MIRI. Okay.

ABRAM. Never, ever leave me.

MIRI. I won't. I promise.

ABRAM. Because you love me?

(**MIRI** *can't say anything and backs away, embarrassed. She nods.*)

(*Definitively.*) You love me. We're in love.

(**ABRAM** *exits this moment. He stands elsewhere onstage.* **MIRI** *watches him.* **MIRI** *sits on a bench;* **RUTH** *enters and sits next to her.* **ESTHER** *enters and sits or stands in front of them.*)

(They are at worship, still in the past. They whisper.)

RUTH. Miri, don't be scared.

MIRI. I'm not scared.

RUTH. Then what is it?

MIRI. I'm... I'm... I can't breathe.

RUTH. *(Taking MIRI's hand.)* It's okay. This is what God wants.

MIRI. I can't feel my...my...face.

ESTHER. *(Harshly.)* Quiet, girls. Do you want everyone to stare at you?

MIRI. Everyone *is* starin' at me.

ESTHER. BE. QUIET.

MIRI. I don't think I can. Ruth, I don't think I can.

RUTH. It's okay. He'll confess, and we'll forgive him, and it'll be over.

MIRI. I want it to be over. I want it to be over.

RUTH. Sit tight.

MIRI. I don't want you to hear this. I don't want Dat to hear this. Where is Dat?

ESTHER. With te men, of course. Hush.

MIRI. Ruth. Ruth, I think I'm goin' blind.

ESTHER. You're not goin' blind, you silly girl.

MIRI. I am. I am.

RUTH. It's okay, Miri. I'm here. I won't let you go blind. Just listen to him. And then forgive. And everythin' will be like it was.

MIRI. You think so?

ESTHER. *(Very angry.)* SHUT. YOUR. MOUTHS. It's time.

    *(**ESTHER** and **RUTH** exit.)*

    (Shift -> The Present.)

    (As indicated by a sound and light cue.)

    *(**ERIC** enters, carrying a tray of biscuits. They are on the porch.)*

MIRI. *(Frantic, alone.)* Ruth? RUTH? MAMA?

ERIC. They're not there.

MIRI. *(As though seeing him for the first time.)* What?

ERIC. No one's here but me. There are biscuits if you want one for breakfast.

> (**ERIC** *holds out the pan to her and sits down on the porch.)*

Do you mind if I eat with you?

MIRI. *(A little surprised, but hiding it.)* Whatever.

> *(They eat in silence for a moment.)*

ERIC. *(Referring to her Amish plainclothes.)* That's a good look on you.

MIRI. Shut up. *(Brushing crumbs from her dress.)* I've forgotten how to eat like a human. A week on the porch was all it took, I guess.

ERIC. *(Joking.)* Yeah, have some class. It's like you were raised on a farm or something.

> *(She smiles at him. A moment of silence.)*

So where is everyone?

MIRI. Oh. Yeah. They must've gone to worship. They'll be gone all day.

ERIC. They didn't go last Sunday.

MIRI. Amish worship every other Sunday. So.

ERIC. Where's the church?

MIRI. They meet in homes and barns. "The God who made the world and all things in it, does not dwell in temples made with hands." When a congregation starts to get too big, they split it. And each congregation has its own bishop, and its own deacons, and its own rules about every single tiny thing. That's called the *Ordnung*. It's different from the Bible, because they make it up as they go along.

ERIC. Gotcha.

MIRI. You really don't know too much about all this, do you? Obsessed as you are.

ERIC. I'm not obsessed.

MIRI. Oh please. You're an addict. If you'd hit a car full of Hare Krishnas, you'd have shaved your head by now.

ERIC. I know enough to know I want to stay here.

MIRI. For how long?

ERIC. Forever. If they let me.

MIRI. You know enough to make that call? You have a real three-dimensional perspective?

ERIC. This is a trap.

> (**MIRI** *launches into a speech she has given many times before, to English acquaintances who ask her, "How could you have ever left the Amish?"*)

MIRI. So you know they only give their kids an eighth-grade education, and that women basically have no rights at all, and that divorce is inconceivable, so if you pick the wrong person when you're nineteen, good luck with THAT for the rest of your life. Oh, and, when crime happens here, they don't retaliate, they don't go to the police, they just turn their backs and wait for it to happen again. Your old life must have been really fucked up to make this place look like the promised land.

ERIC. *(Pause.)* I wrote copy at this marketing firm in Philly. That was my job. Making people believe that they needed things. Trying to copyright words like "happiness." It upset me. A lot. I was drinking all the time. Every night, until I passed out. It wasn't fun, it wasn't social, it was just... I couldn't imagine a day without it. I had to escape from all of my stupid, indefinable non-problems. I felt ridiculous because I was miserable and I didn't know why I was miserable, and I didn't have a thing to be, because everyone I knew was just what they were "doing," and what I was "doing" made me so sad. I started coming in late. Doing a crappy job. Got fired. Drank more. My girlfriend, Alexis, told me I couldn't love her because I didn't love myself. Well, I didn't love myself AND I didn't love

Alexis, BUT I don't know that the two things were related. Not directly.

MIRI. Okay, okay.

ERIC. You can't tell me a bunch of bad stuff out of context to try to scare me off, because I've seen bad stuff. Lots of it. But I've never seen this kind of good stuff. Your dad's always saying, "Everything is wonderful." And he means it.

MIRI. "Everything is wonderful" is code in this family.

ERIC. For what?

MIRI. For "shut up."

ERIC. *(Puzzled.)* That can't be true.

MIRI. You're not purging any of your demons by hiding out.

ERIC. Yeah, but I am. This is not the first time I've been in recovery, Miri. But this is the first time I actually don't want to jump off the wagon. All the things that people said to me before, about how much clearer and happier I'd be if I quit drinking – I'm actually starting to believe them.

MIRI. Whatever you can't deal with out there, it will eventually find its way in here.

ERIC. *(In a mock-therapist voice.)* You have a lot of anger.

MIRI. Yes. And it's the only thing that's kept me from walking into traffic some nights.

ERIC. But you can be a clean slate here.

MIRI. There are different rules for you, than for me.

ERIC. Speak, forgive, forget.

MIRI. Don't the Catholics have that, too?

ERIC. Technically. Except God forgives you, but no one else does. I want to confess before the whole congregation.

MIRI. No one really forgives. They say they do, but it's not forgiving. It's pretending. I know it's very appealing to you, but this code allows people to get away with horrible things. Then everyone has to act like the whole mess is invisible. And if you can't, if you want to stand up and say, "I'm hurt, I'm disappearing, I'm not okay, I want to talk about this," then you have to go away.

With nothing. The guilt connects you like a bruise you can poke on, but the door is shut and locked. And then you're out there, walking down the street in the city, looking at all the people, and it hits you one day: every single one of them has to make some kind of life. There is no plan. There is no right answer. And there is no help on the way.

ERIC. The last time I was in rehab, I had this moment. My parents had forced... *(No...)* They were really worried. It was the best thing, maybe, but it wasn't my idea.

MIRI. Yeah.

ERIC. And I was in a group session, and the woman leading the session said in her real soft voice, "You can all get better, because you can choose to be well." And I immediately heard my own voice say, in my head, "No, I can't. I don't have any control over that." And I knew I was going to drink again, as soon as I got out of there.

MIRI. I really hate when people say you have a choice, when you actually don't.

ERIC. Yeah, but I do. I mean, it's a choice I would have to make every single minute for the rest of my life, but... I'm beginning to think I might actually be able to do it. It's not about just waiting it out.

MIRI. Because time doesn't fix anything.

ERIC. Exactly.

MIRI. Exactly.

(A beat between them.)

I need your help.

ERIC. Woof. I'm barely putting one foot in front of the other right now, sister.

MIRI. You have a seat at the table. Inside.

ERIC. Yeah?

MIRI. If you hear anything about Ruth. Anything *at all* that sounds like marriage talk, you have to tell me. Immediately. Understand?

ERIC. Ruth's like a kid!

MIRI. Ruth is eighteen, and she's baptized. Abram is old for a bachelor. Things move very, very quickly around here, and they are almost irreversible once they get going. Everyone pretends that Abram's perfect, but he's possessive. He's pushy.

ERIC. He doesn't have me fooled.

(*JACOB and ABRAM enter. They are deep in conversation in a barn, post-worship. They are cleaning up after the service.*)

ABRAM. I enjoy the company of men. Get along well with men. But all men need a solid partner.

ERIC. I don't like that guy any more than you do, Miri, but it's not exactly my place to tell your little sister who she can and can't marry.

MIRI. (*Gravely.*) Ruth only wants to make everyone happy. Abram will ruin her.

ABRAM. There is somethin' very warm and sincere about Ruth. A very solid, promisin' young woman.

MIRI. I'm half of what's left. They're my family, and I didn't fight for them last time. Please? For Ruth?

ERIC. (*Short pause.*) I'll let you know what I hear.

(*MIRI crosses to ERIC and hugs him, or perhaps just touches his shoulder in thanks. ERIC exits; they are both a little embarrassed. ESTHER enters across the stage and begins cleaning egg off the side of the barn. MIRI watches her.*)

ABRAM. And I think I know what kind of man Ruth wants – a man with solid values. A man who knows his place in the community.

JACOB. A humble man.

(*MIRI crosses to ESTHER and begins to help her mother clean the side of the barn. This is a few days earlier, immediately following the scene in which she put back on her Amish plainclothes. They work in silence.*)

ABRAM. Yes. Forgive me. I am too eager to make my point.

JACOB. You're sayin' you're interested in marryin' our Ruth?

ABRAM. I know the timin' seems strange, but perhaps a celebration would help us all to move on from our grief. Levi and Joshua were almost brothers to me. I could care for their sister. Perhaps that is God's will.

JACOB. We can only see God's will revealed after te fact.

ABRAM. I believe I'm still unmarried because it's God's will. I thought I had a very specific future, with...with Miri. Once. But that was not the case. I have opened myself up to atonement and trusted in God's plan, and until now I haven't found anyone who moved my heart. Perhaps that was a penance for me, from Him. To be alone. Until now.

JACOB. *(Pause.)* Ruth is sweet. Te sweetest child I've ever known. Joyful. Honest. I'm so happy to know her, and so scared at the same time. I'm scared for her, te same way I'm scared when I see a butterfly flyin' around a group of rowdy kids. Afraid that life will...bruise her. She has no brothers, anymore, and I'm not as strong as I was. Not goin' to live forever. And her sister... All these things are hard on her.

> *(The barn is clean.* **ESTHER** *exits without speaking to* **MIRI.** *After a moment,* **MIRI** *follows her.)*

ABRAM. I'll take care of Ruth. If you let me, Jacob.

JACOB. *(Pause.)* You have my permission to continue to court our Ruth. Let's save marriage talk for another day.

ABRAM. But, if Ruth should start to talk marriage? If she were the one to bring it up?

JACOB. Go and sit with her, Abram. At the singin'. Don't ask any more of me today.

> *(***ABRAM** *exits, searching for* **RUTH. RUTH** *enters, at his back; he does not see her. She is carrying a pile of clean laundry.* **ESTHER** *enters from the other side of the stage and*

crosses to **RUTH**; *she watches* **ABRAM** *as he exits. They are in the living room.)*

ESTHER. Bring those here. Are they dry?

RUTH. Yes. I just took them off the line.

ESTHER. Let's fold them now before they wrinkle. Supper can wait a few minutes.

RUTH. I can do this myself, if you need to tend to supper.

ESTHER. No, no, no, Ruth. "Many hands make light the work."

(They fold sheets in silence for a moment.)

RUTH. What is it, Mama?

ESTHER. What is what?

RUTH. What do you want to talk to me about?

ESTHER. What gives you te idea tat I want to talk to you about anythin'?

RUTH. Because when you're this quiet, you are pickin' your words.

ESTHER. Ah. *(Pause.)* Ruth, what do you think of Abram?

RUTH. Miri's Abram?

ESTHER. He doesn't belong to Miri.

RUTH. That's still how I think of him.

ESTHER. That is not how he thinks of himself.

RUTH. Oh. *(Pause.)* He's a good worker. All the families rely on him. He's always first to help. I think one day that God will choose him to become a deacon, or even the bishop.

ESTHER. I think you're right.

(A short silence between them.)

RUTH. Is that all you wanted to ask me?

ESTHER. No. Ruth, how do you feel about Abram as a man?

RUTH. As opposed to...as a fish?

ESTHER. Don't make jokes. This is a serious conversation I'm tryin' to have with you.

RUTH. Why?

ESTHER. Why am I tryin' to talk to you?

RUTH. Why does it matter what I think of Abram?

ESTHER. Don't be foolish, Ruth. You know he's sweet on you.

RUTH. I don't think so. I think he's just tryin' to cheer me up, about Levi and Joshua.

ESTHER. It's more than tat, child. He has talked to your dat.

RUTH. About me?

ESTHER. Your dat has told me that Abram wants to marry you.

> (**ERIC** *enters, unseen. He cannot understand the conversation; they are speaking in German.*)

RUTH. *(Shocked.)* But...but. It's only been... It's not even a month since we buried them.

ESTHER. I know. I am not tryin' to rush you. I am not tryin' to force you. I want to know what you think about the man.

RUTH. I told you what I think. He is a good Amish man and everyone relies on him.

ESTHER. But could you marry him?

RUTH. I don't know that I can, Mama.

ESTHER. Because of Miri.

RUTH. I don't know that I can marry anyone. I don't want to be married yet. I want to stay here and take care of you and Dat.

ESTHER. That's no life for a young girl. And who will give us grandchildren?

RUTH. Maybe Miri.

ESTHER. English children. Wouldn't be ours.

RUTH. I can be strong, too. I can be here. I want you to look at me like you used to look at Miri. It's my job to keep us together.

ESTHER. We're a family, Ruth. God will keep us together.

RUTH. He has done a lousy job of that.

ESTHER. What was that?

RUTH. *(Quietly.)* Nothing. *(Conceding.)* Abram does make me laugh sometimes. That's a nice thing.

> *(A short pause.* **ERIC** *coughs to get their attention.* **ESTHER** *turns and sees him.)*

ESTHER. Oh, it's you, Eric.

ERIC. Yes, ma'am. I was wondering if I could help in any way with dinner?

ESTHER. Why don't you set te table?

ERIC. I can do that.

ESTHER. And set an extra place, please. Abram will be joinin' us tonight.

ERIC & RUTH. Abram?

ESTHER. Yes. Please set a place for Abram.

> *(***ERIC** *exits.)*

(Pause.) When your father and I started courtin', I was a little younger than you. My mother was dead. Your dat was soft-spoken, like my father. I had known his sister for years. But it made things hard for my family, when he took me away.

RUTH. Mama –

ESTHER. *(Interrupting.)* It was te right thing, tat's what I'm tellin' you. *(Short pause.)* Your dat had not done *Rumspringa*. He had raised his brothers and sisters. I had raised mine. We never got to talk to each other, before, not really, not about really personal things. I liked him, but I didn't really know him. And he made things hard for our family. *(Pause.)* Your father talks too much sometimes and he has dark moods. But he's kind, and patient. We are partners, and I know tat te work I do matters. The last few weeks...I would have broken into a thousand pieces without him. *(Pause.)* You can never know at te beginning. But it was clearly God's will, for us. Think about God's will for you.

RUTH. *(Pause.)* Yes, Mama.

(Lights up on **MIRI** *on a different part of the stage; she is in the barn.* **ERIC** *rushes in.* **ESTHER** *exits to the kitchen and begins to work on supper.* **RUTH** *folds the last sheet and follows her mother off.)*

MIRI. What? What happened?

ERIC. Your mom and your sister. I overheard them talking.

MIRI. What did they say?

ERIC. I don't know! They were speaking German! But it sounded serious. And Abram's coming for dinner.

MIRI. Abram's coming for dinner?

ERIC. Your mom told me to set a place for him.

MIRI. *Abram* is going to eat with my family?

ERIC. That is what I'm telling you. Yes.

MIRI. Unbelievable!

ERIC. Believe it. He's probably already here.

*(***MIRI** *is furious. She begins to pace.)*

What do you want me to do?

MIRI. Kill him.

ERIC. What do you really want me to do?

MIRI. You said you would help.

(Silence. What can she tell him? Maybe she's helpless against this, after all.)

ERIC. I gotta go set the table.

*(***ERIC** *exits.* **MIRI** *paces for a moment, then freezes. She is still in the barn. She sees* **ABRAM** *approaching before we do and her whole body stiffens.)*

(Shift –> The Past.)

(As indicated by a sound and light cue.)

(It is the day after the end of Act One, five years ago.)

MIRI. Shut up.

(**ABRAM** *enters.*)

ABRAM. I haven't said anythin'.

MIRI. Don't talk.

ABRAM. What's wrong with you?

MIRI. What's wrong with me?

ABRAM. That's what I'm askin'.

MIRI. (*Trying to initiate an impossible conversation for which there is no language.*) Last night...

ABRAM. Don't worry. I won't tell. You're actin' so strange, Miri.

MIRI. No. Don't say my name. I won't say your name.

ABRAM. (*Approaching her.*) Are you feelin' guilty? It's okay. I told you it's okay. I'm goin' to be your husband, and you have to follow where I lead.

MIRI. I don't – I didn't...want to...

ABRAM. You did want to. You kissed me. You told me you'd marry me. You wanted to. (*Pause.*) You're scared because it was a sin. I know it was a sin. But be scared of God, not me.

(**ABRAM** *walks toward her.*)

MIRI. Stop.

ABRAM. I don't understand.

MIRI. No. You don't. And I don't know how to make you.

ABRAM. Do you still love me?

(**MIRI** *is silent.*)

Miri, do you still love me??

(**MIRI** *is silent.*)

I love you. I would never hurt you. I would kill anyone who tried to hurt you.

MIRI. Then kill yourself.

ABRAM. (*Very hurt.*) You don't mean that.

(*Beat.* **ABRAM** *makes a decision.*)

I'll confess. I'll tell the bishop.

MIRI. You'll go in front of the whole town and say what you did?

ABRAM. That will make you love me again.

MIRI. No! That...that won't –

ABRAM. *(Interrupting.)* That's the best way.

MIRI. I'll have to sit and listen. That will kill me.

ABRAM. Don't be vain.

MIRI. Vain?

ABRAM. I love you, but you're vain.

MIRI. I'm not! I'm not vain, I'm...

> *(She puts her head in her hands. She can't do this anymore. She deflates.* **ABRAM** *crosses to her.)*

ABRAM. It's all goin' to be okay. I'll fix this.

> *(**ABRAM** wraps his arms around **MIRI**. She stiffens.* **ABRAM** *kisses her, not tenderly, but possessively and desperately. She does not kiss him back. He pulls away. She slaps him, hard. They stare at each other for a long moment.)*

(Holding his face.) You'll want to make confession for that.

> *(**ABRAM** exits. **MIRI** is alone in the barn.)*
>
> *(Shift –> The Present.)*
>
> *(But the past hangs all around.)*
>
> *(As indicated by a sound and light cue.)*
>
> *(Lights up on the kitchen. The table is set for six.* **RUTH** *and* **ESTHER** *enter and sit.* **ERIC** *and* **JACOB** *enter and sit.)*
>
> *(**MIRI** does not exit. She turns and looks at the kitchen. Her place at the table is set, but empty.* **ABRAM** *enters and sits next to* **RUTH**.)*
>
> *(**RUTH, ABRAM, ERIC, ESTHER**, and **JACOB** join hands and bow their heads to pray.* **MIRI** *is ready to explode.)*

JACOB. Heavenly father, we thank you for this meal. Please bless te earth tat gave it and te hands tat prepared it. We thank you for our friends and family gathered here today –

>   (**MIRI** *bursts into the kitchen.*)

MIRI. (*Interrupting.*) No! NO. This will not happen. He will not eat in here while I stand out there. He will not hold Ruth's hand. I don't accept this. You'll have to kill me.

ABRAM. (*Standing, trying to remain calm.*) Miri, you're makin' a scene.

MIRI. Get out! GET OUT OF HERE!

ABRAM. (*Venomously, losing his cool.*) YOU get out! You are NOT WANTED HERE!

MIRI. It's your fault they're dead!

ERIC. (*Bowing his head.*) I –

MIRI. (*Pointing at* **ESTHER** *and* **JACOB.**) YOUR FAULT! This is your punishment! For, for pushing me out and forgetting me! God took Levi and Joshua to punish you for what you did to me, and you KNOW IT. That's why you can't LOOK AT ME! You say you forgive people, but you don't, you just replace people!

ERIC. (*Standing.*) Maybe we should all just calm down.

ABRAM & MIRI. (*To* **ERIC.**) YOU shut up!

>   (**ESTHER** *jumps to her feet, angrier than we have ever seen her.*)

ESTHER. (*Screaming.*) SILENCE!

>   (*The room is quiet. It is totally shocking for a good Amish woman to behave this way.*)

This is my home. This is my family. My home. MY LIFE.

>   (*A silence.*)

>   (*More quietly.*) The three of you. Get out.

ABRAM. Jacob?

ESTHER. (*Raging again.*) I SAID GET OUT OF MY HOUSE.

>   (**MIRI** *and* **ABRAM** *exit.* **ERIC** *hangs back.*)

ERIC. What did I do?

ESTHER. *(Defeated.)* You just don't belong. You don't belong
to us.

> (**ERIC** *exits, on the verge of tears.)*
>
> *(Lights dim on the kitchen.)*
>
> *(There is a sound and light cue to indicate
> transition into the next movement.)*

Scene 6: Speak   *My monologue!*

(The Present.)

(Several hours later. Lights up on the barn. **MIRI** *is sitting alone.)*

(Lights up on the kitchen. **ESTHER** *enters and begins cleaning up the uneaten supper dishes.)*

*(**MIRI** prays.)*

MIRI. God?

God – question mark?

> *(**MIRI** shakes her head and closes her eyes for a moment, then changes tactics.)*

Levi? Joshua?

I don't know if I believe in heaven anymore, but I believe you're there. Can I do that?

Can I just believe in a heaven for you?

A heaven where the fields are already plowed and the cows are already milked and the chores are all already done and worship is already over when you wake up, and all there is left to do is take long walks and tell scary stories and lie in the sunshine after swimmin' in the small lake, like we did on Sunday afternoons.

And eat Mama's biscuits and go for buggy rides with Dat, and listen to Ruth sing, quietly, only for the four of us.

Can there be a heaven like that?

And will you wait for me there?

I think I can do better, for the rest of my life, if I can make myself believe you're waiting for me there.

Oh, help. Oh.

I always thought eventually they'd forgive me for leavin'. And you'd forgive me for leavin'. And I wouldn't live here again, not ever, but I'd come for Christmas. And I'd see your little dark-haired babies and laugh with your wives. And we'd be a family. And it wouldn't always be "with us or against us," but just, sometimes, like once a year, just "us."

But you're both dead.

I'm alive, and I'm here...

I just thought we had time.

> (**JACOB** *enters the kitchen and watches* **ESTHER.** *After a moment, he speaks.*)

JACOB. Are you feelin' better now?

ESTHER. I'm feelin' fine.

MIRI. Dat can't keep lovin' me if I don't stay. Mama can't even look at me.

And our sweet Ruth...if she marries Abram, I'll lose her, too.

JACOB. Tell te truth to me, Esther.

ESTHER. *(Pause.)* No.

JACOB. I don't know what to say to you.

ESTHER. Well good. Because I wouldn't know what to answer.

> (*A beat between them.*)

MIRI. I have this...thing... I can't relax. I can't sleep.

Am I crazy?

I went to a therapist, you know, out there.

She told me I'm not crazy. But I'm not out there.

And here, if you can't breathe and you can't sleep, somethin's simply wrong between you and God.

ESTHER. I frighten you.

JACOB. No.

ESTHER. I do.

JACOB. *(Pause.)* Yes. Sometimes.

ESTHER. Like my mother frightened my father.

JACOB. *(Concerned.)* Are you tryin' to tell me somethin'? Do you mean to...

ESTHER. No! No... No.

JACOB. Good. I couldn't bear this without you.

ESTHER. I don't know if I can bear this at all.

> (**JACOB** *takes* **ESTHER***'s hand.* **MIRI** *exits. Perhaps she mumbles the same prayer her father prays, under her breath.*)

JACOB. "I will lift up mine eyes unto te hills,
From whence cometh my help.
Behold, he tat keepth Israel
Shall neither slumber nor sleep.
Te Lord shall preserve thee from all evil:
He shall preserve thy soul."

ESTHER. *(Quietly.)* What if te evil is not outside us, but inside?

JACOB. *(Earnestly.)* You are not evil. Never say tat. We are all upset. Tat does not make us evil.

> (*Lights up on* **ERIC** *and* **RUTH** *on the porch at the same time as the other scene onstage.* **RUTH** *is returning to* **ERIC** *his wallet, phone, and watch.*)

ERIC. Thanks. Man, these feel so weird to me now. You should keep them.

RUTH. *(Shaking her head.)* I don't have need of 'em.

ERIC. I guess it's weird I'm still wearing these clothes, huh? I came out here to change them. But...I hate my old clothes.
(Picking up his phone.) I have missed this...
(Overwhelmed.) Ugh. I just can't do this right now. I can't make all these changes at once. I was doing so well.

ESTHER. I carried them in my arms. Her. Miriam. I named her. You named te others. I named her for rejoicin'. I had such hope for her. My girl.

JACOB. You still love her.

ESTHER. How could I stop?

JACOB. She needs to know tat.

RUTH. You're more peaceful now, Eric. You can take that with you, wherever you go.

ERIC. I don't think I can, Ruth. When I think about getting on a bus, going back to the city...I feel the tunnel closing around me.

RUTH. The tunnel?

ERIC. It shuts out everybody but me.

ESTHER. Miri made a choice. She –

JACOB. *(Interrupting.)* No. We made a choice. To ignore te fact tat she was dyin' under our roof.

ESTHER. She wasn't dyin'.

JACOB. Her spirit was dyin'. Now she's so dark inside. Sour. Have you heard her laugh, once, since she got here? Nothin' like the girl we knew. We failed her. We let her drift out into te world with nothin'.

ESTHER. Tat is te *Ordnung*.

JACOB. Te laws are meant to bring us closer to God. To protect us from temptation and worldliness. Not to divide us. Not to turn our children bitter and afraid.

> *(ESTHER releases JACOB's hand.)*

ESTHER. She's a stranger. I've lost her.

JACOB. She needs you still.

ESTHER. She needs God.

JACOB. How can she believe that God will not forsake her, if you already have?

> *(ESTHER hears him. It is a blessing. ESTHER and JACOB exit.)*

ERIC. *(Harshly, angry at himself.)* Why did I ever think it was okay to come here? I'm such an idiot.

RUTH. You were meant to come to us, Eric. You can't think all this time has been wasted.

ERIC. Your sister was right. I didn't *discover* anything. I was just hiding. And now it's all going to be the same, isn't it? *(Pause, then an outburst.)* I want a drink so goddamn bad! Sorry.

RUTH. *(Pause.)* Do you have a sister?

ERIC. *(Pause.)* Yeah.

RUTH. When you look at me, it's like you're lookin' for somebody else. You should go to her.

ERIC. She doesn't want to see me.

RUTH. Yes she does.

ERIC. You don't know her.

RUTH. I don't have any brothers anymore. I'm not sayin' that to make you feel bad. Just to make you realize you're takin' someone else's brother from her, too.

> *(Lights up on* **MIRI** *in the barn, in her English clothes. It is the next morning. She is packing.)*

ERIC. I wish I could have your voice inside my head all the time, Ruth. I think I'd sleep better.

RUTH. It's not my voice you're wantin', Eric. It's His.

> *(Lights down on the porch. It is now the morning after* **ESTHER** *kicked everyone out of the house.)*

> *(***ABRAM** *enters the barn. He turns to go when he sees* **MIRI**, *but she stops him.)*

MIRI. Abram!

ABRAM. I was lookin' for your father.

MIRI. He's in the house.

ABRAM. I'll go. *(He turns to leave.)*

MIRI. Wait. Please?

> *(Something in her tone makes him turn around.)*

ABRAM. Did you say "please" to me?

MIRI. Don't walk away.

ABRAM. Why not? That's what *you* did.

MIRI. *(Calmly.)* You say that like you're not the reason I had to leave.

ABRAM. You didn't have to leave. You chose to leave. I'm so tired of bein' blamed for your choices.

MIRI. What choices did I have? Stay here and be pitied, gossiped on? How could I see you every day, not even able to talk about it?

ABRAM. You gave me somethin'. And then you took it back.

MIRI. You thought I owed you.

ABRAM. I thought you *loved* me. I thought God's will was for us to be together.

MIRI. What's the difference between God's will and your will?

ABRAM. On my best days, there is no difference.

> *(A tense silence between them.)*

Are you a good person, Miri?

MIRI. *(Defensively.)* I –

ABRAM. *(Interrupting.)* I know you're a *wronged* person. I know you're a *wounded* person. But are you a good person?

> *(**MIRI** stares at him. She opens her mouth, then shuts it.)*

MIRI. I should know the answer to this.

> *(The question has pulled her up short. She takes a long moment to think before she speaks again.)*

I don't know. I don't know if I do any things that are good, if I make the world a better place in any real way. I'm good at my job. I pay my rent on time. I don't steal or murder or lie, any more than anyone else lies. But I don't know if all that stuff adds up to a good person. I don't even know how to know. *(Pause.) Ruth* is a good person. *Dat* is a good person. If you asked them they would say they aren't, but that's what good people say. But is it even really goodness, if you have no other choice?

ABRAM. *(Quietly.)* I don't know.

MIRI. I have a lot of choices now. I have a lot of freedom. I can do whatever I want. And the price of that is being completely alone.

(*Beat.*)

Are you a good person, Abram?

ABRAM. (*Pause.*) I'm a person that people say good things about.

(*A beat.*)

MIRI. (*Pause.*) I would have married you.

ABRAM. (*Sadly.*) You're a liar. You lied then and you're lyin' now. You never would have married me. You never would have stayed here. I knew you'd leave me, from the moment I met you.

MIRI. I met you when I was four years old.

ABRAM. I knew.

(*A beat.*)

MIRI. (*A discovery.*) Is that why you did it? To keep me here?

ABRAM. (*Quietly.*) I was afraid.

MIRI. Did you think God was on your side that night?

ABRAM. Yes. I think I did.

(*Beat.*)

MIRI. Have you...since?

ABRAM. Haven't you?

MIRI. No.

ABRAM. Maybe you should.

MIRI. I don't have those feelings. I try, but I don't. (*Pause.*) You do.

ABRAM. Yeah.

MIRI. With who?

ABRAM. English girls.

MIRI. Where do you meet English girls?

ABRAM. In bars sometimes. I wear English clothes. I don't have a beard; they don't know who I am.

MIRI. That must be nice.

ABRAM. It is. I don't have to be extra perfect, because they don't know the worst thing I ever did.

>   *(A beat.)*

MIRI. Ruth is not me as I might have been.

ABRAM. I know that, now. *(Pause.)* I miss you so much.

MIRI. Please don't do that.

ABRAM. How long can you hold on to this, Miri? Everyone knows what I did. It hangs like a cloud over my life. I went in front of everyone, and I made confession. I did that for you. I was willin' to do anythin' to fix what I broke.

MIRI. You made that confession for yourself.

ABRAM. For YOU! I asked for forgiveness, and everyone forgave.

MIRI. You didn't ask *me*.

ABRAM. What?

MIRI. You didn't ask for *my* forgiveness.

ABRAM. The whole town...

MIRI. Ask me.

ABRAM. Now?

MIRI. Now.

ABRAM. *(Pause.)* Miriam. I'm sorry you got hurt.

MIRI. That's not the same as "I'm sorry I hurt you."

ABRAM. It's the best I can do.

>   *(**ABRAM** exits. **MIRI** continues to pack in silence in the barn.)*

>   *(Lights up on the kitchen, also in the present, on a different part of the stage. **RUTH** is clearing breakfast dishes. **ESTHER** is taking them from her and washing them.)*

>   *(**RUTH** picks up two clean plates.)*

ESTHER. Eric didn't come in for breakfast today.

RUTH. He probably thinks you're mad at him.

ESTHER. Why would he think tat?

RUTH. You kicked him out of the house.

ESTHER. He's not ours to save, Ruth. We are not helpin' him by shelterin' him. His problems are out there, waitin'. They are real, and he must be strong enough to face them.

RUTH. We can help to strengthen his will.

ESTHER. We don't strengthen people here. We break them.

(A silence.)

RUTH. Mama...Miri didn't mean what she said last night, about Levi and Joshua. She didn't know what she was sayin'.

ESTHER. She meant it.

RUTH. She still belongs to us. Even if she doesn't belong here.

ESTHER. *(Looking squarely at* **RUTH.***)* Don't hold on to anythin' too tightly, Ruth-girl. If you forget everythin' else I've ever told you, remember tat. You hold to things too tightly, you will crush them.

> *(***MIRI*** *is still sitting in the barn. She has to leave, she knows it, but she's frozen here.)*

RUTH. I'm not goin' to marry Abram, Mama.

ESTHER. No?

RUTH. I'm maybe not goin' to marry anyone. I don't know. But not him. Not just because everyone thinks it would be good. It wouldn't be good. Not for me.

ESTHER. Then you don't have to marry Abram.

RUTH. I don't?

ESTHER. No. Of course you don't.

> *(***RUTH*** *runs over and embraces her mother.* ***ESTHER*** *is surprised, but after a moment she hugs* ***RUTH*** *back.)*

RUTH. God bless you, Mama.

ESTHER. God bless you, Ruth.

(Lights dim on the kitchen.)

*(After a moment, **ERIC** enters the barn. He begins to pack in silence and **MIRI** watches him. He has a beat-up old bag and some care package items given to him by the family.)*

(A beat.)

MIRI. Will you go back to Philly?

ERIC. Oh. No, I don't think so. I want... *(No...)* I need to be somewhere quieter, I think.

MIRI. Do you have someone to stay with?

ERIC. I'll figure it out.

MIRI. Because you probably shouldn't live alone. If you get lonely, and you get in your head again –

ERIC. I said I'll figure it out, Miri.

(A pregnant silence.)

MIRI. I live on a quiet street.

ERIC. What?

MIRI. I mean, in the city, but the neighborhood is quiet. Close to buses. And there's a weekly AA meeting at a YMCA about two blocks away. A friend of mine goes. She could take you.

ERIC. What exactly are you saying?

MIRI. It's probably not as nice as where you're used to living, but...I want you to come stay with me. I want you to figure it out. I believe you can.

ERIC. This is a bad idea.

MIRI. No, it's a good idea. It's what a good person would do.

ERIC. I can't.

MIRI. Why not?

ERIC. *Why?*

MIRI. You need a friend now. And so do I.

ERIC. Are we friends?

MIRI. Aren't we? *(Pause.)* I have this knot inside me, like, behind my sternum, and it's just been there for five years, and I've learned to just, like, breathe *around* it. It's like a rock. It's like a tumor. And I didn't realize how hard it had gotten to breathe until...just now. But I feel it getting...looser. And you're part of that. *(Pause.)* We can't have this life, *(She gestures to the barn, the community.)* but maybe we don't have to be totally alone, either.

ERIC. So that's what's in it for you.

MIRI. Please take me seriously. I'm really trying here.

ERIC. Yeah. So am I. *(Pause.)* Okay. Thank you.

> *(A short pause. A beginning.)*

MIRI. There's a bus soon. You all packed?

ERIC. Do you think we can stay until worship on Sunday? I still want to confess.

MIRI. Why is that so important to you?

ERIC. Because someone told me I've had many blessings. And I'm trying to believe in that.

> *(JACOB enters.)*

Will you be there?

MIRI. I'm not exactly wanted.

ERIC. I want you there.

> *(We jump forward in time. JACOB crosses to ERIC. Two lights come up onstage. A large one in the center, around MIRI. A smaller one downstage; ERIC crosses to it, led by JACOB.)*

> *(The rest of the play is presentational, metaphorical, a demonstration of gratitude. Even tragedies can end in gratitude. The audience should be completely included and the fourth wall, if one still exists, should fall away.)*

JACOB. We're not usually this mixed up, about te past and te present. Our lives are pretty clear. But when te accident happened, it's like a hole opened up and te past crawled through.

MIRI. Speak, forgive, forget.

JACOB. You don't have to make confession to earn our forgiveness.

ERIC. Not trying to earn it. Just trying to accept it.

(Another small light comes on downstage, opposite **ERIC***'s.* **ABRAM** *enters and crosses to it.* **ABRAM***'s light signifies that he is in the past;* **ERIC** *is in the present. The three lights form a triangle onstage.)*

(Watching **ABRAM***.)* His shoulders aren't really all that impressive.

*(***ERIC** *and* **ABRAM** *are about to make their public confessions.* **MIRI** *watches both of them.* **ESTHER** *enters and crosses to* **MIRI***. They are in the present. The rip in time that began tearing the moment* **MIRI** *left, and burst wide open when Levi and Joshua died, is knitting itself back together in this moment.)*

ESTHER. *(Behind* **MIRI***.)* You can't expect Abram to understand. Men don't feel things te way we do.

MIRI. *(Not turning around.)* No one feels things the way you and I do, Mama.

ESTHER. Forgiveness is the spine of life.

MIRI. I'm tryin', Mama. I'm out of practice.

ESTHER. *(Pause.)* You could practice on me.

MIRI. What do you mean?

ESTHER. Listen to me with an open heart. For practice.

MIRI. Okay.

ESTHER. Miriam. I am sorry for what I took from you.

MIRI. You're sorry?

ESTHER. I should have protected you. I should have fought for you. But I was ashamed. I was afraid and ashamed.

MIRI. I can't...

(**RUTH** *enters.* **RUTH** *crosses to* **MIRI** *and takes her hand.* **JACOB** *stands behind* **ABRAM** *but watches* **MIRI** *and* **ESTHER**.)

ABRAM & ERIC. All of you know why I'm here.

ABRAM. I have moved away from God.

ESTHER. And now there is a distance between us tat has swallowed all te affection. And I'm callin' out to you from across this divide, but I don't know te words tat will make you hear me.

MIRI. These are the words. I hear you.

(**MIRI** *begins to break down.* **JACOB** *watches her.*)

ESTHER. I love you. Always. Even when I want you to think I don't. I'm lovin' you where you can't see.

(**ESTHER** *puts her hand on* **MIRI**'s *shoulder. Touching her excommunicated daughter, in front of the whole congregation, is a huge deal.* **ESTHER** *is choosing* **MIRI** *over the Ordnung.*)

ERIC. I fucked up. (*Embarrassed at his language.*) I mean, I messed up.

ABRAM. I'm afraid.

ERIC. I'm lost.

ESTHER. I am here to surrender and be forgiven.

RUTH. (*Looking at* **MIRI**.) It's time.

MIRI. I want to forgive you. That will be some good in the world. All the good I know how to do.

ABRAM & ERIC. My actions have brought pain to everyone here.

ABRAM. And I regret them.

ABRAM & ERIC. I made a family suffer.

ERIC. A good family.

ABRAM. I hurt the person I love most in the world. And I think I've lost her.

Please.

ABRAM & ERIC. Forgive me.

ERIC. I never thought that anything I did could affect so many people. I'm sorry I found out this way.

> *(A beat.)*

> *(**MIRI** watches her father. This is his chance to be on her side.)*

> *(**JACOB** crosses to **MIRI**, breaking the Amish rules that separate men and women. **JACOB** takes her hand.)*

ABRAM. There's nothin' that can heal the hurt, except maybe time, and that might make it worse. I'm here because I am responsible for her life, and for that hurt. And for this darkness.

> *(**JACOB** kisses **MIRI** on the head.)*

I'm here. In the light. I surrender.

> *(Lights go out on **ABRAM** and **ERIC**. After another moment, lights go down on the family.)*

> *(Blackout.)*

End of Play

Everything Is Wonderful

William M. Golden, 1918
Luke 10:33-34

A Beautiful Life

Each day I'll do _____ a gold - en deed, _____ By help - ing those _____ who are in need; _____ My life on
To be a child _____ of God each day, _____ My light must shine _____ a - long the way; _____ I'll sing His
The on - ly life _____ that will en - dure, _____ Is one that's kind _____ and good and pure; _____ And so for
I'll help some - one _____ in time of need, _____ And jour - ney on _____ with ra - pid speed; _____ I'll help the
While go - ing down _____ life's wear - y road, _____ I'll try to lift _____ some trav - 'ler's load; _____ I'll try to

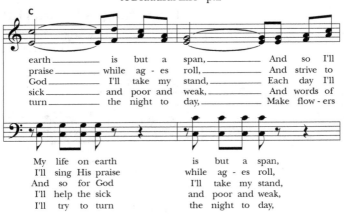

Upper vocal line:
earth	is	but	a	span,	And	so	I'll
praise	while	ag -	es	roll,	And	strive	to
God	I'll	take	my	stand,	Each	day	I'll
sick	and	poor and	weak,	And	words	of
turn	the	night	to	day,	Make	flow - ers

Lower vocal line:
My	life	on earth	is	but	a	span,
I'll	sing His praise	while	ag -	es	roll,
And	so	for God	I'll	take	my	stand,
I'll	help the sick	and	poor and	weak,
I'll	try	to turn	the	night	to	day,

C/G   Am G7   C

do	the	best	I	can
help	some	trou - bled	soul.
lend	a	help - ing	hand.
kind -	ness	to	them	speak.
bloom	a -	long	the	way.

And	so	I'll	do	the	best	I	can
And	strive	to	help	some	trou - bled	soul.
Each	day	I'll	lend	a	help - ing	hand.
And	words	of	kind - ness	to	them	speak.
Make	flow - ers	bloom	a -	long	the	way.

REFRAIN   C   F/C   C   F

Life's eve-ning sun,   Is sink-ing low,

Life's eve-ning sun, _____ Is sink-ing low, _____ A few more